The Big Book
OF SCRAPBOOK PAGES

500+ New Designs for Capturing All Your Memories

Edited by Kelly Biscopink

MEMORY
MAKERS
BOOKS

Memory Makers Books
Cincinnati, OH
www.memorymakersmagazine.com

The Big Book of Scrapbook Pages. Copyright© 2011 by Memory Makers Books. Manufactured in USA. All rights reserved. No part of this book may be reproduced in any form or by any electronic or mechanical means including information storage and retrieval systems without permission in writing from the publisher, except by a reviewer who may quote brief passages in a review. Published by Memory Makers, an imprint of F+W Media, Inc., 4700 East Galbraith Road, Cincinnati, Ohio, 45236. (800) 289-0963. First Edition.

15 14 13 12 11   5 4 3 2

Distributed in Canada by Fraser Direct
100 Armstrong Avenue
Georgetown, ON, Canada L7G 5S4
Tel: (905) 877-4411

Distributed in the U.K. and Europe by F+W International
Brunel House, Newton Abbot, Devon, TQ12 4PU, England
Tel: (+44) 1626 323200, Fax: (+44) 1626 323319
E-mail: postmaster@davidandcharles.co.uk

Distributed in Australia by Capricorn Link
P.O. Box 704, S. Windsor, NSW 2756 Australia
Tel: (02) 4577-3555

Library of Congress Cataloging-in-Publication Data

The big book of scrapbook pages : 500+ new designs for capturing all your memories / edited by Kelly Biscopink. – 1st ed.
      p. cm.
   Includes index.
   ISBN-13: 978-1-59963-133-2 (pbk. : alk. paper)
   ISBN-10: 1-59963-133-4 (pbk. : alk. paper)
   1. Photograph albums. 2. Scrapbooking. 3. Photographs–Conservation and restoration. I. Biscopink, Kelly
   TR465.B54 2011
   745.593–dc22

2010040276

www.fwmedia.com

Editor: Kelly Biscopink
Writer: Courtney Walsh
Designer: Corrie Schaffeld
Production Coordinator: Greg Nock
Photographer: Christine Polomsky

Metric Conversion Chart

to convert	to	multiply by
Inches	Centimeters	2.54
Centimeters	Inches	0.4
Feet	Centimeters	30.5
Centimeters	Feet	0.03
Yards	Meters	0.9
Meters	Yards	1.1
Sq. Inches	Sq. Centimeters	6.45
Sq. Centimeters	Sq. Inches	0.16
Sq. Feet	Sq. Meters	0.09
Sq. Meters	Sq. Feet	10.8
Sq. Yards	Sq. Meters	0.8
Sq. Meters	Sq. Yards	1.2
Pounds	Kilograms	0.45
Kilograms	Pounds	2.2
Ounces	Grams	28.3
Grams	Ounces	0.035

A NOTE FROM THE EDITOR

As scrapbook artists, we're all unsure of how to lay out a certain page from time to time. But we have also experienced the moment when we realize we've created a wonderful piece of art that encapsulates not just memories, but emotions as well. These are the times of artistic breakthrough that keep us coming back to scrapbooking as a way of expressing ourselves through our art.

This book is filled with hundreds of inspiring layouts, all created by readers of Memory Makers books and website, that we know will help spark your creativity. These 500+ layouts were chosen because of unique and beautiful designs, enticing storytelling or wonderful photos. We received thousands of entries, and we thoroughly enjoyed looking through all of them.

Some of the layouts in this book will remind you of moments you've been trying to capture in your scrapbook, and others will have you grabbing for your camera to go make some new memories!

Thank you to all the contributors who have made this book possible. Your art is an inspiration to all of us!

Happy scrapping!

Kelly Biscopink

Table of Contents

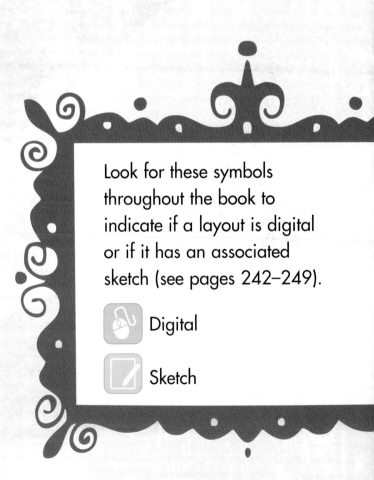

Look for these symbols throughout the book to indicate if a layout is digital or if it has an associated sketch (see pages 242–249).

Digital

Sketch

INTRODUCTION

Feeling stumped? Frustrated? Stuck in a creative box? Lost your mojo? Bored? In desperate need of...something?

Let's face it. We all need inspiration. Ideas. Ways to fill up our creative tank. Even the most artistic person in the world needs to rest and recharge. You probably picked up this book looking for a new idea. After all, ideas come at us in the most surprising ways. Something jumps out at us in the grocery store. An overheard conversation in the doctor's office gets your mind whirling. Your child does something unexpected, like slowing down for a minute, touching your face and telling you he loves you.

In those moments, a story starts to form in your mind. You have the perfect photos to tell the story. But when you sit down to scrap it, the ideas aren't there. Maybe you're caught up on the photo placement. Maybe the colors have tripped you up. Whatever it is, this book can help. Think of it as fuel for your creative gas tank. This isn't a book to flip through at random. It's a book to sit down with, to enjoy, perhaps with a notepad and a pen and over an uninterrupted cup of coffee. It's a book that will help you find new and interesting topics, unique layouts and different techniques.

These pages will give you countless new things to try—things that will keep you excited to scrapbook, anxious to tell your stories and eager to try something new. If you're tired of feeling like something is missing, you're in good hands. In these pages, you'll find just the inspiration you've been searching for.

Courtney Walsh
Writer, scrapbook designer and author

Chapter One:

EVERYDAY MEMORIES

Christmas. Birthdays. Graduations. Anniversaries. Special events easily find their way into our scrapbooks. But most of the hours in our days aren't spent celebrating holidays. Our lives are made up of the minutes between the sunrise and the sunset. The hobbies that bring us joy. The faith that gives us hope. We plan entire scrapbooks around special events, but it's the simple, everyday moments that truly enrich our lives. This chapter will inspire you to start looking for the little things you want to remember—the moments that define your days. And don't stop at all things pretty. Life is messy—there's no reason to hide it. Document a laugh, a schedule, your child's meltdown in the grocery store...be sure to include all of the daily activities to provide a complete picture of this life you are living.

What A Wonderful Life

Amy Tan
Culver City, CA

Supplies: Cardstock, stickers, rub-on numbers (American Crafts); patterned paper (American Crafts, Scrap in Style TV, Scarlet Lime, Hambly, DCWV); trim (Flair Designs); leaf (Prima); Misc: pen, vintage cards, tags

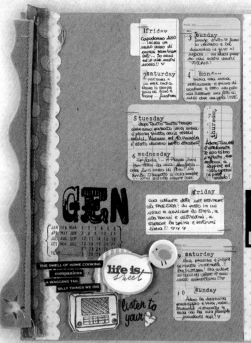

Inspired Idea!

Document all of your favorite everyday memories on one layout by using a numbered key. Adhere all of your photos in a tight design on one side of your layout and then create journaling blocks to describe each one. Making the journaling blocks a part of your design enables you to include more words to adequately describe each special memory.

Everyday Memories

Loredana Bucaria
Quarto Napoli, Italy

Supplies: Patterned paper (Daisy D's, American Crafts); stamps (Sausan Designs, CatsLife Press, Prima, Hero Arts); stickers (Fontwerks); letters (Making Memories, American Crafts); embellishments (American Crafts, Tattered Angels, Fancy Pants, Heidi Swapp); paper trim (Fiskars); Misc: old book paper, fabric, black ink pad, black glittery embossing powder, punch, cardboard, pen

Relax

Ellen Sosnoski
Paxinos, PA

Supplies: Cardstock (Bazzill); patterned paper (Black Market Paper Society); chipboard pieces (Jenni Bowlin, Chatterbox); letters (Chatterbox, American Crafts); felt (American Crafts); jewels (Glitz); spray inks (Tim Holtz); Misc: digital sun design (free download), doily, fabric tag from jeans, marker

Picking Flairs

Nicole Martel
Crownsville, MD

Supplies: Cardstock (Bazzill); patterned paper (Pink Paislee, Lily Bee); flower (Prima); rub-ons (BasicGrey); glitter mist (Tattered Angels); ink (Ranger); stamps (Tim Holtz); bling (Creative Imaginations); punches (Martha Stewart Crafts, EK Success); button (Autumn Leaves)

Box Of Love

Donna Jannuzzi
San Diego, CA

Supplies: Cardstock (Bazzill); patterned paper, letters, sticker, flower (Jillibean Soup); trim (Doodlebug); button (Prima); snaps (Paper Source); Misc: punch

Platinum Pinktallica

Andrea Friebus
La Habra, CA

Supplies: Cardstock (American Crafts, Bazzill); patterned paper (Fancy Pants, My Mind's Eye, MAMBI); grommets, die-cut machine (Making Memories); stickers (My Little Shoebox); die-cut trim (Bazzill); brads (Oriental Trading Company); Misc: ink, punch

PLATINUM

There is no name for my favorite color of metallic pink, so I have decided to call it "platinum pinktallica." I cannot get enough of this color and have already collected two cameras, a watch, a phone, and an ipod in this luscious hue. Next on the list…a metallic pink car!!

Everyday Strife

Jing-Jing Nickel
Roseville, MN

Supplies: Patterned paper, chipboard elements (Cosmo Cricket); stickers (Cosmo Cricket, SRM Press); letters (American Crafts); Misc: pen

Snapshots

Meg Barker
Detroit Lakes, MN

Supplies: Patterned paper (Crate Paper, Little Yellow Bicycle, Love Elsie); chipboard frames (Li'l Davis); flower (Making Memories); jewel (Paper Studio); journaling cards (October Afternoon); letters (American Crafts); paper trim (Anna Griffin); stickers (7gypsies); Misc: pen, letters

Life As I Know It

Kim Frantz
(Memory Makers Master, 2009)
Downingtown, PA

Supplies: papers, mask used with photo by Vinnie Pearce (Designer Digitals); stitches (Anna White), buttons, tape (Designer Digitals); worn page edges (by Lynn Grieveson for Designer Digitals, Two Little Pixels); Misc: Bickham Script font, Batik Regular font (downloads from the Internet)

Angel Kisses

Lydia Wiley
Ozawkie, KS

Supplies: Patterned paper, tags (BasicGrey); letters (American Crafts, BasicGrey); Misc: pen

I Love Your Silly Faces

Becky Williams
Wolfforth, TX

Supplies: Patterned paper; journal spot (Cosmo Cricket); stickers (Jenni Bowlin, American Crafts, Adornit); buttons (Sassafras Lass)

So Cute

Pamela Young
Thornton, CO

Supplies: Patterned paper, letters, flowers, gems (Prima); Misc: 3D paint, floss, Lucinda Handwriting font

A Day Without Laughter...

Katie Saylor
San Antonio, TX

Supplies: Cardstock (Bazzill); patterned paper (BasicGrey, BoBunny, October Afternoon, Sassafras Lass); letters (American Crafts); Misc: punch

Stain Glass Do-Over

Connie Hyde Mercer
Belmont, TX

Supplies: Cardstock (Bazzill); patterned paper (Jenni Bowlin); letters (American Crafts, Making Memories); journal paper (Jenni Bowlin); ticket (Jenni Bowlin); Misc: buttons, handmade flower, ink, border punch

First Load

Melanie Smith
Conception Bay South, Newfoundland

Supplies: Cardstock (Bazzill); patterned paper (Cosmo Cricket, BasicGrey); letters (BasicGrey); flowers (Hero Arts); journaling spot (October Afternoon); button (BasicGrey); label maker (Dymo)

Everyday Life

Beckie Curtis
Eaton Rapids, MI

Supplies: Software (Adobe); background paper by Katie Pertiet, patterned paper, date tag, wordart, template (Designer Digitals)

Inspired Idea!

Next time you want to create a photo strip using several same-sized photos, save yourself a little time! Pull the photos into a photo editing program (like Photoshop), size them on the computer and add a decorative digital frame. Print all photos as one block and simply cut the entire block and adhere it to your page as you would one large photo! Quick and easy!

Our Morning Routine

Jill Surginson
Kanata, Ontario

Supplies: Cardstock (Bazzill); patterned paper (October Afternoon, Scenic Route); letters (American Crafts, Making Memories); frame (Scrapbook-Bytes); stickers (October Afternoon); Misc: ink, border punch, pen, button, Century Gothic font

Garage Sale

Glenda Tkalac
Moose Jaw, Saskatchewan

Supplies: Patterned paper (My Mind's Eye); letters (Pressed Petals, Colorbök); die-cuts (Jillibean Soup); gel pen (MultiCraft Imports)

The 1943 House

Christa Paustenbaugh
Camp Lejeune, NC

Supplies: Patterned paper (Studio Calico, Scenic Route); chipboard elements (Maya Road); letters (BasicGrey); stickers (Studio Calico); flowers (Crate Paper, Making Memories); felt accent (American Crafts); metal key (Making Memories); stamp (Studio Calico); Misc: ribbon, ink

46 Hours

Laura Achilles
Littleton, CO

Supplies: Cardstock (Bazzill); patterned paper (BasicGrey); letters (American Crafts); adhesive (Helmar); chipboard frames (American Crafts); fleece flowers (American Crafts); sticker (Sassafras Lass); buttons (BasicGrey); ribbon (Creative Imaginations); Misc: punch, ink, paper doily, floss

Cookie Dough

Brenda Hurd
Plain City, UT

Supplies: Cardstock (Kraft); patterned paper (BasicGrey); letters (American Crafts); spoons (BasicGrey); buttons (BasicGrey); Misc: glitter mist, ink, corner punch, border punch

KS

Donna Jannuzzi
San Diego, CA

Supplies: Cardstock (Bazzill); patterned paper (Studio Calico); letters (American Crafts); flowers (Maya Road); pearl flower accent (Jenni Bowlin)

My Little Baker's Man

Donna Jannuzzi
San Diego, CA

Supplies: Cardstock (Bazzill); patterned paper (Jillibean Soup); letters (BasicGrey, Jillibean Soup); stickers (Jillibean Soup); metal clip (Stampin' Up); Misc: punch

Shakes

Ellen Sosnoski
Paxinos, PA

Supplies: Cardstock (Core'dinations); patterned paper, felt button (Chatterbox); chipboard heart (Magistical Memories); letters (American Crafts); butterfly strip (Chatterbox); bling (Heidi Swapp); stamp (myStamp BOX); Misc: rick rack, ink, notebook punch, Arial font

Coolin'

Wendi Manuel-Scott
Leesburg, VA

Supplies: Cardstock, die-cuts (Studio Calico); patterned paper (BasicGrey, Studio Calico); letters (American Crafts, Making Memories); paper elements (Sassafras Lass); flower centers (Prima)

There Is A Mouse In My Pantry

Wendy Kwok
Singapore

Supplies: Patterned paper (Sassafras Lass); letters (American Crafts); stickers (My Little Shoebox)

Looking for a way to incorporate tons of cool embellishments and still maintain a clear focal point? Next time, try cutting an oversized frame (like the patterned paper circle shown here). With all elements positioned to touch the frame and lead the eye toward the photo, the picture becomes the star!

First Grade

Nicole Stark
(Memory Makers Master, 2007)
Roy, UT

Supplies: Cardstock (Bazzill); patterned paper (Cosmo Cricket, Studio Calico, October Afternoon); envelope (Maya Road); library card, paperclip (Making Memories); letters (American Crafts, Cosmo Cricket); die-cuts (Provo Craft); Misc: buttons, pen, floss, journaling spots

Back To School

Pamela Young
Thornton, CO

Supplies: Patterned paper (Creative Imaginations, Cosmo Cricket, Studio Calico); stickers (Creative Imaginations); letters (My Little Shoebox); Misc: floss

Our Little School Boy

Erin R. Wells
Elsmere, KY

Supplies: Patterned paper (Cosmo Cricket, Sweetwater, We R Memory Keepers); chipboard heart (Heidi Swapp); letters (Jenni Bowlin, Making Memories); tab sticker (Creative Imaginations); tag, ribbon (Cocoa Daisy); tickets (SEI); buttons (Autumn Leaves, Cocoa Daisy, SEI, Stampin' Up); pencils (Cosmo Cricket); Misc. ink, pen, punch, staples

Fashion Savvy

Carol Monson
Las Vegas, NV

Supplies: Cardstock (Bazzill); patterned paper (Sassafras Lass, October Afternoon, Studio Calico); letters (American Crafts, Sassafras Lass); chipboard (Maya Road); tag (Sassafras Lass); Misc: acrylic paint, brad, ink, pen

Just Got My Ears Pierced

Jill Paulson
Yankton, SD

Supplies: Cardstock (DCWV); patterned paper (Heidi Swapp, We R Memory Keepers); letters (Making Memories); decorative edge punch, scallop trimmer, heart punch (Fiskars); Misc: American Typewriter font

Extra! Extra!
ONE SKETCH, THREE WAYS

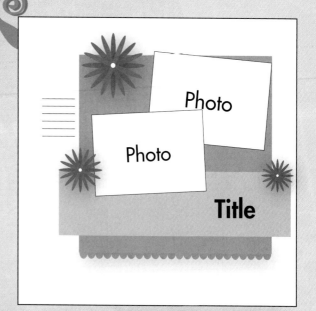

These three layouts, all based on this sketch, show you how take a sketch and stretch your inspiration to create multiple pages.

I Reply

Andrea Friebus
La Habra, CA

Supplies: Cardstock (American Crafts, Bazzill); patterned paper (Creative Imaginations, K&Co); transparency (K&Co); brads (Karen Foster); stickers (Paperchase, Making Memories, Hambly, American Crafts); brads (Making Memories); Misc: pen, punch, thread, fabric

Take A Pic

Kelly Goree
(Memory Makers Master, 2006)
Shelbyville, KY

Supplies: Cardstock (My Little Shoebox); patterned paper (Making Memories); letters, stickers, buttons, brads (BasicGrey); acrylic paint (Plaid); chalk ink (Clearsnap); Misc: pen, adhesive, jute

My Dream

Jamie Warren
Rentz, GA

Supplies: Patterned paper (Cosmo Cricket, Studio Calico); letters (American Crafts, BasicGrey); photo stickers (3M); adhesive dots (Therm O Web); create a sticker (Xyron); embellishments (Prima)

Inspired Idea!

Who says you need a photographer to take your portrait? Set your camera up on a tripod, use the timer and ham it up for the camera all on your own! The best part of taking your own portraits is you can be as silly as you want to be and no one will ever know. What better way to document your personality?

Today At 30

Loredana Bucaria
Quarto Napoli, Italy

Supplies: Patterned paper (American Crafts, La Fourmi Creative, Scenic Route); chipboard (American Crafts); stamps (Catslife Press, Banana Frog); stickers (7gypsies, BoBunny, Fontwerks); letters (Scenic Route, American Crafts, Making Memories); embellishments (La Fourmi Creative, Making Memories, BasicGrey); Misc: pen, package paper, old book paper, black ink, black embossing powder

Little Pink Houses

Beth Price
Westfield, IN

Supplies: Cardstock (Stampin' Up); patterned paper (BoBunny); die-cut paper (BasicGrey); border punch (Stampin' Up, EK Success); chipboard house (Scenic Route); flowers (BasicGrey); stamp (Hero Arts); ink (Stampin' Up); letters (October Afternoon, American Crafts); gem (Prima); Misc: embossing powder, adhesive foam

I grew up on a farm. So my idea of living with people is a little different from the lifestyle we lead. Sometimes I yearn for space, not these side-by-side "Little Pink Houses" that all look alike and go right down the row. It's a love/hate relationship. I love that you girls have friends to play with all the time. I hate that my garden is little and that when we're in the yard, we're on display. But it's something to be thankful for. We have a lovely house in a wonderful neighborhood. And isn't that the American dream? Ain't That America?

Her Laugh

Lynn Warner
Coal Valley, IL

Supplies: Patterned paper, chipboard shapes, letters (BasicGrey); Misc: circle punch, brown pen, brown ink, ribbon

Work In Progress

Grace Tolman
Garden Grove, CA

Supplies: Patterned paper, stamp, letters, brads (Upsy Daisy); journaling spot (Creative Imaginations); punch (Fiskars); pen (American Crafts); colored pencil (EK Success)

Just One Smile

Cathy La Hay
Lake Villa, IL

Supplies: Cardstock (Bazzill); patterned paper (Graphic 45); letters (Maya Road); rub-ons (Daisy D's, American Crafts, Creative Imaginations); bling, jewels (Doodlebug); ribbon (American Crafts); flowers (Prima); stamps (Stamps by Judith, A Muse); Misc: ink, glitter mist

Own It

Veronica Jennings
Waldorf, MD

Supplies: Cardstock, letters, embellishments (American Crafts); patterned paper (Studio Calico); stamps (Purple Onion) Misc: pen, acrylic paint, spray ink

Inspired Idea!

Looking for a little extra dimension without adding a ton of bulk? Add texture to your next layout by pleating a sheet of patterned paper and adhering only the top of the strip to the layout. This will allow the bottom pleats to pop off the page, but still lay flat in your closed scrapbook album. What a great way to create visual interest on the cheap!

Me.

Jennifer Day
Ottawa, Ontario

Supplies: Cardstock (Bazzill); patterned paper (BasicGrey, Scrap Within Reach, Making Memories, Pink Paislee, Cosmo Cricket); letters (American Crafts, Making Memories, Dollarama); journaling spot (My Mind's Eye); felt (Close To My Heart); ribbon (Close To My Heart, American Crafts); hatpin (Close To My Heart); punch (Martha Stewart Crafts, Stampin' Up, Fiskars); die-cut (Stampin' Up); transparency (7gypsies); bling (Kaisercraft, Recollections, Making Memories); crochet flower (Close To My Heart) Misc: ink, glitter mist

Inspired Idea!

We all love patterned paper, but it doesn't make the best base for hand-written journaling! Next time you need a way to journal and you don't have room in your design for a text box or strips of paper, simply use your finger to apply a coat of acrylic paint to the edges of your page. Then use a pen or marker to write your journaling all around the outside of the layout.

This Is Me

Julie Walton
Simi Valley, CA

Supplies: Patterned paper (Graphic 45); letters (American Crafts, Kaisercraft); stamp (Donna Downey); buttons (Rusty Pickle); bingo card (Jenni Bowlin); stickers (7gypsies); acrylic paint (Plaid, Helmar); punch (Martha Stewart Crafts); Misc: pen, floss, pearl trim

I've Learned

Robyn Schaub
Dallas, TX

Supplies: Cardstock (Paper Studio); patterned paper (Making Memories, Scarlet Lime); chipboard (Chatterbox); letters (American Crafts); i-Top brad-maker (Imaginisce); jewels (Imaginisce); Misc: ink, punch, pen, adhesive

Spotlight On...

Courtney Walsh
Rockford, IL

Courtney Walsh
is the author of *The Busy Scrapper* (Memory Makers Books, 2008). With *The Busy Scrapper*, you can scrap fast and hassle free! Packed with tips and techniques showing you how to scrap in a flash, this book is a one-stop guide to efficient layouts that are fun to make. Visit Courtney at www.courtneywalsh.typepad.com.

Reminder
Supplies: Patterned paper (BasicGrey); Misc: ribbon, Courier New font

Peter Pan
Supplies: Organic kit (Shabby Princess); Misc: Georgia font

Inspired Idea!

A really cool artifact from the past is worth including even if it adds a little extra bulk to your scrapbook. For this layout featuring an old kindergarten photo and report card, the addition of the personalized pencil (held onto the page by embroidery floss) is not only a cool design element, but a sentimental one as well.

Kindergarten

Yvette Adams
Banks, Australia

Supplies: Patterned paper (American Crafts, KI Memories, Jenni Bowlin); letters (October Afternoon, Jenni Bowlin); rub-ons (Hambly); flower (Heidi Swapp); Misc: bookpaper, pencil, circle punch, trim, chipboard, button

My View-Master Life

Lynn Warner
Coal Valley, IL

Supplies: Patterned paper, journaling stickers (October Afternoon); letters (American Crafts); tape (7gypsies); spinner (Tim Holtz); T-pin (Making Memories); Misc: black pen, brown ink, vintage View-Master slide and sleeve

37 Weeks

Nicole Martel
Crownsville, MD

*Supplies: Patterned paper, chipboard, rub-ons
(BasicGrey); bling (Creative Imaginations); lace (Prima)*

I Count

Grace Tolman
Garden Grove, CA

*Supplies: Cardstock (The Paper Company); patterned paper
(Upsy Daisy); acrylic paint (Plaid); border punch (Fiskars); letters
(American Crafts); pen (Zig); Misc: string*

This Makes Me Happy

Serena Gedlaman
Calgary, Alberta

*Supplies: Cardstock (Scenic Route); patterned paper (BasicGrey);
letters (We R Memory Keepers); transparency (Fancy Pants),
buttons (BasicGrey); flowers (Making Memories); rub-ons
(BasicGrey); Misc: ribbon, pen, border punch*

Spotlight On...

Jessica Acs
Victoria, British Columbia

Jessica Acs
is the author of *Outstanding Mini Albums* (Memory Makers Books, 2009). In this book, you'll get inspiration, techniques and step-by-step projects for 50 fabulous mini scrapbooks. You'll see that showcasing your biggest memories is easy with adorable mini albums. Visit Jessica at www.jessicaacs.com.

Living My Dream

Supplies: Patterned paper (Bazzill, Fancy Pants, Sassafras Lass, Jillibean Soup); cardstock stickers (Sassafras Lass); letters (American Crafts, October Afternoon); journaling squares (October Afternoon); Misc: pen, ink

Pieces Of Me

Supplies: Patterned paper (7gypsies, Scenic Route); letters (October Afternoon, American Crafts, Making Memories); cardstock stickers (BoBunny); tickets (Jenni Bowlin); Misc: ink

Conquer

Terri Hayes
Cary, NC

Supplies: Cardstock (Bazzill); patterned paper (Cosmo Cricket, Sassafras Lass); thickers, ribbon (American Crafts); stickers (My Little Shoebox); epoxy (Clearsnap); ticket (Tim Holtz); Misc: pen, clip

You Have The Courage...

Noeleen Acosta
Pasadena, CA

Supplies: Cardstock (Bazzill); patterned paper (Graphic 45); letters (Making Memories); bling (Prima); ribbon, stamp, chipboard flourishes (Rusty Pickle); clip (7gypsies); Misc: pen, thread, staples, glitter

Going The Distance

Katharyn Brine
Murrumbateman, New South Wales

Supplies: Software (Adobe Photoshop Elements 6); cardstock, patterned paper (Three Paper Peonies); scroll (Kaisercraft)

A Dream Come True

Linda Sobolewski
Guilford, CT

Supplies: Patterned paper (Tinkering Ink, October Afternoon); thickers (American Crafts); letters (Pink Paislee); stamp set (Studio Calico); ribbon (American Crafts); stickers (Jenni Bowlin); Misc: brad, staples, punch, pen, ink

Soar

Melyssa Connolly
Harmony, Nova Scotia

Supplies: Software (Adobe); digital elements (The Digichick)

Faith

Juliet Adora Concepcion
Renton, WA

Supplies: Cardstock (WorldWin); patterned paper (BasicGrey, K&Co, Making Memories); transparency (Making Memories); letters (QuicKutz)

Welcoming Change

Amy Martin
(Memory Makers Master, 2009)
Corpus Christi, TX

Supplies: Software (Corel PaintShop Photo Pro); patterned paper, wordart, bird, frame, stamp, staples (Oscraps); Misc: 1942 Report font

Inspired Idea!

We are used to making lists. To-do lists to keep us on task. Pro-and-con lists to help us visualize the answer to a big decision or life change. Honey-do lists to gently remind our spouses the weekend isn't just for relaxing! Why not take that affinity for list-making to the scrapbook page by creating simple, easy lists to act as concise journaling that will add something special to every page?

I Believe In...

Nancy Doren
Colorado Springs, CO

Supplies: Cardstock (unknown); patterned paper (K&Co, GCD Studios, My Mind's Eye); jewels (Prima); letters (American Crafts); Misc: punches, thread, Batik Regular font

Faith Plan 2010

Gina Johnson
Mt. Carmel, IL

Supplies: Patterned paper (Lily Bee); chipboard brackets (Maya Road); letters (American Crafts, Jenni Bowlin, My Little Shoebox); rub-ons (Lily Bee); pearls (Kaisercraft); journaling (Microsoft Word, Dymo); Misc: butterfly punches, curly label punch, double loop punch, close to cocoa ink, journaling pen

I couldn't believe it when the sales lady at J.C. Penny measured your foot and told me you needed a size 14 shoe! And here I thought you were just trying to keep up with your older brother that had just grown into size 13. When you kept on complaining that the next size was still too small, I pulled in the reinforcements to call your bluff ~ but it was true! I felt terrible for doubting you but still...that's 2 REALLY BIG feet!

August 20, 2008   size 14

2 Big Feet

Cindy Wick
Tacoma, WA

Supplies: Cardstock (The Paper Company, Bazzill); letters (Creative Memories, Making Memories)

Bearded Boy

Stephanie Wheeler
Chattanooga, TN

Supplies: Cardstock, patterned paper (BasicGrey); letters (American Crafts); chipboard shape (Maya Road); stickers (BasicGrey, Sassafras Lass); stamp (7gypsies); Misc: pen, ink, handmade button, typewriter, thread

every winter, the beard comes back.
i love it at first, then i start to miss
his chin. i know he'll shave eventually,
then winter will come
and it'll start all over again.

The Real You

Nina Pateña

Pasig, Metro Manila, Philippines

Supplies: Cardstock (Bazzill, Papemelroti); patterned paper (Little Dreamer Designs); overlay (Hambly); die-cut (Crate Paper); Blue Streak Mixed Media Kit, foreign text (Gauche Alchemy); stickers (7gypsies, American Crafts); software (Microsoft Image Viewer); Misc: sequin waste, gauze paper, cardboard, staples, ink, pen

Inspired Idea!

A great way to put all attention on your photo is by creating a visual triangle with your embellishments. The three stitched orange stars on this page do just that. By repeating the same shape and color three times in three different sizes, then positioning in a triangle around the photo, the eye is naturally drawn to just the spot it should be.

What I Like About You

Nancy Doren
Colorado Springs, CO

Supplies: Cardstock (unknown); patterned paper (Lily Bee); stickers (American Crafts, Jenni Bowlin); Misc: font, thread, jewels

Work Enthusiast

Connie Hyde Mercer
Belmont, TX

Supplies: Cardstock (Bazzill); patterned paper, journal card (Jenni Bowlin); calendar card (Jillibean Soup); letters (American Crafts, Jenni Bowlin); ticket (Jenni Bowlin); Misc: buttons

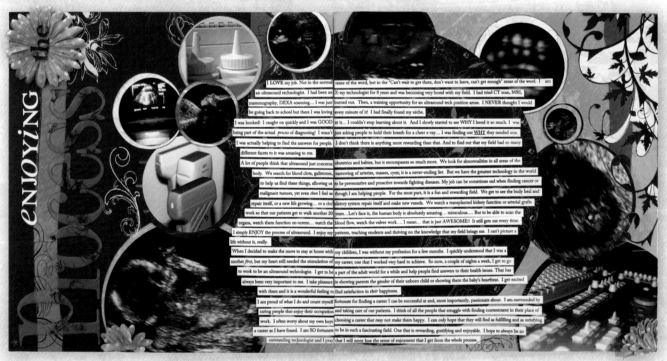

Enjoying The Process

Kristin Hayne
Castle Rock, CO

Supplies: Cardstock (Bazzill); patterned paper (Rouge de Garance); rub-ons (BasicGrey); letters (Heidi Swapp, Making Memories); flowers (Petaloo); jewels (My Mind's Eye); chalk (Clearsnap); Misc: Adobe Caslon Pro font, Willing Race font

Back To Work

Yvette Adams
Banks, Australia

Supplies: Cardstock (KI Memories); patterned paper (Fancy Pants, Sassafras Lass); rub-ons (Making Memories, BoBunny); journaling spot (Making Memories); Misc: pen

Inspired Idea!

Life isn't always lemonade. Sometimes you have nothing but a bowl of sour lemons. It's important (and maybe a little therapeutic) to document the bad and ugly along with the good. Even a tongue-in-cheek look at something you aren't crazy about—pet peeves, daily routines, anything that puts a knot in your stomach—is worth getting in your scrapbook. It's everyday life, after all!

Hang In There

Glenda Tkalac
Moose Jaw, Saskatchewan

Supplies: Patterned paper (Imagination Project); die-cuts (Maya Road, Imagination Project, Chatterbox); stickers (Imagination Project, Making Memories); brad (Make it Special); acrylic paint (Making Memories); marker (American Crafts)

Blue

Cindy Stevens
Saint John, New Brunswick

*Supplies: Cardstock (Prism, The Paper Company); papers
(Pink Paislee, Creative Imaginations); die-cut paper
(Making Memories); pearl bling (Kaisercraft);
letters (American Crafts); rub-ons (Pink Paislee);
Misc: office clip, ribbon, buttons*

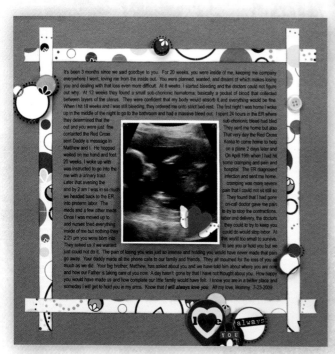

Love You Always

Brianne Nevill
Fort Lewis, WA

*Supplies: Cardstock (Bazzill); patterned paper (Cosmo Cricket);
brads, adhesive foam, button (American Crafts); chipboard element (CherryArte); letters (Adornit); rub-ons (Scenic Route);
Misc: scissors, glitter, pen, punch, ink, Arial font*

Alone Time

Chrys Q. Rose
Tracy, CA

*Supplies: Cardstock (Bazzill); patterned paper (SEI); jour-
naling spot (Making Memories); chipboard (BasicGrey);
metal brads, buttons (Boxer Scrapbook); stickers (Making
Memories); letters (American Crafts); Misc: glitter*

Spotlight On...

Michele Skinner
Burnsville, MN

Michele Skinner
is the author of *Your Words, Your Story* (Memory Makers Books, 2008). With the book, learn to tell your story as no one else can. Get writing with journaling prompts, layout ideas and solutions to common journaling problems.

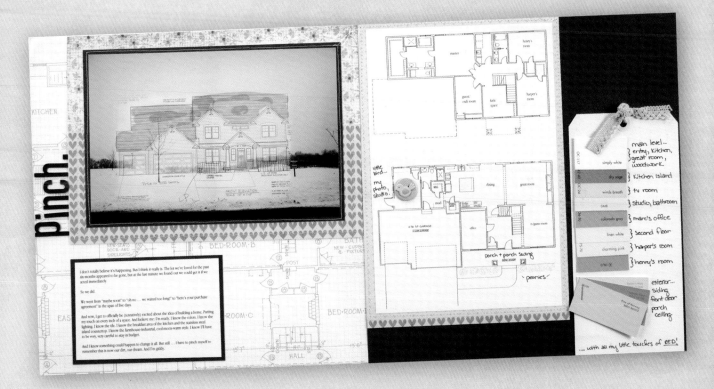

Pinch

Supplies: Cardstock (Bazzill); patterned paper (Avery, Studio Calico, BasicGrey); adhesive (American Crafts); chipboard button (Maya Road); letters (American Crafts); mailing label (Avery); brad (Doodlebug); Misc: pen, colored pencils

Creative Art

Denise C. Lofts
Lenexa, KS

Supplies: Cardstock (Bazzill); letters (American Crafts); rub-ons (My Mind's Eye); soft charms (KI Memories); staples (EK Success); Misc: stickers

From Scratch

Grace Tolman
Garden Grove, CA

Supplies: Cardstock (DCWV); patterned paper, brads (Upsy Daisy); letters, pen (American Crafts); journaling spot (Creative Imaginations); punch (Fiskars); Misc: thread, sewing machine

This picture was taken March 2007. William had just installed my new cabinets. It looks more cluttered & "used" 3-years later, but it's "my space." My space to come & let creativity take over. Sometimes it's not so creative & sometimes I surprise myself. But that doesn't really matter. It's my place to get lost from the outside world, housework, homework & the stress from daily life. I love that I have my own place to get away & couldn't imagine it not being here. I'm so thankful we were able to incorporate my space into the floor plans of our house.

my space

My Space

Dawne Ivey
Cantonment, FL

Supplies: Patterned paper (Studio Calico, BasicGrey); letters (American Crafts); buttons (BasicGrey); rhinestones (Kaisercraft); scallop scissors (Fiskars); Misc: machine stitching, Tahoma font

For Me

Stephanie Wheeler
Chattanooga, TN

Supplies: Cardstock (BasicGrey, Collage Press); patterned paper (K&Co, BasicGrey, Cosmo Cricket); letters, brads (BasicGrey); chipboard shapes (American Crafts); pearls (Kaisercraft); Misc: pen, glitter mist

for me

You are 5-years old & in kindergarten.
You already know how to read.
THAT just blows my mind.
Because you're in a private school,
you have the advantage of a good education.
I love to sit & listen to you sound out your letters
& read sentences to me.
And most of all, YOU enjoy reading.
You love it so much, you want to read
the same book to us over & over again.

Read

Dawne Ivey
Cantonment, FL

Supplies: Cardstock (Bazzill); patterned paper (Sassafras Lass, Studio Calico); letters (American Crafts); appliqué (Offray), scallop scissors (Fiskars); Misc: machine stitching, alphabet border sticker, Tahoma font

Inspired Idea!

An online journal isn't just for grandma to see cute pictures of your kids. Your blog is a wonderful documentation of your day-to-day life and a great way to add journaling to your pages. Next time you're stumped for details, check your blog for the nitty-gritty and add them to your layout. You'll have the whole story to accompany your photos in no time.

Library Love

Ann-Marie Morris
Simi Valley, CA

Supplies: Cardstock (DCWV); patterned paper (Pebbles, October Afternoon, American Crafts); letters (BasicGrey); pins (Maya Road); rhinestones (Darice); Misc: pen, buttons, doilies, punches, staples, thread

Top 15 Tunes

Nicole Martel
Crownsville, MD

Supplies: Cardstock (Bazzill); patterned paper (Webster's Pages); thickers (American Crafts); letters, sequins, ribbon, acrylic paint (Making Memories); adhesive foam (EK Success); heart punch (Creative Memories)

Just A Wii Bit Obsessed

Suzanna Lee
Glen Allen, VA

Supplies: Cardstock (Bazzill); patterned paper (Sassafras Lass, Reminisce); letters (American Crafts, Making Memories); photo corner (Heidi Swapp); Misc: punch, pen

Join The Party

Staci Etheridge
(Memory Makers Master, 2008)
McKinney, TX

Supplies: Cardstock (Bazzill); patterned paper (Hambly); stickers (American Crafts, Thoip); transparency frame (Colorbök); Misc: acrylic paint

Sheer scrapbooking embellishments can add so much to your layout—especially when you repurpose them. Instead of simply adhering them to your page, consider tracing the design directly onto your cardstock background and then coloring it in with watercolor pencils. This gives your embellishment the chance to pull double duty and makes a really cool addition to any page!

Embrace The Moment

Ria Mojica
Pasig, Metro Manila, Philippines

Supplies: Cardstock (Bazzill); patterned paper (Teresa Collins); sheers (Maya Road); rub-ons (7gypsies, Fancy Pants, Jenni Bowlin); acrylic corner (Pageframe Designs); letters (Around the Block); Misc: pen, watercolor pencils, ink

Picture This

Kristine Ponte
Abbotsford, British Columbia

Supplies: Cardstock (Bazzill, Core'dinations); patterned paper (Cosmo Cricket); flower die-cut (Sizzix); letters (October Afternoon); buttons (Studio Calico); doily rub-ons (Hambly); vintage calendar tag (Elle's Studio); Misc: pen, embroidery floss, sewing machine, ink

Miss Music

Tricia Gorden
South Bend, IN

Supplies: Patterned paper (Kaisercraft); letters (Fancy Pants, Pink Paislee); rhinestone embellishments (Zva Creative); Misc: acrylic paint, glitter mist, ink

Inspired Idea!

Nothing is off-limits when it comes to your scrapbook layouts—not even the packaging your chipboard alphabet letters came in. The letter casing can serve as a unique, recycled mask. Simply place it over a sheet of white cardstock and spray it with watered-down paint and glitter mist. Use a fine-tipped marker to outline the letters for a fun, handmade look.

Favorite Past Time

Wendi Manuel-Scott
Leesburg, VA

Supplies: Cardstock (Studio Calico, American Crafts); patterned paper (BasicGrey, Sassafras Lass); die-cut (Making Memories, Sassafras Lass); flowers (American Crafts, Sassafras Lass); rubons (American Crafts); glitter mist (Tattered Angels); acrylic paint (Making Memories); brads (BasicGrey); Misc: baker's twine

Music Lover

Yvonne Yam
Singapore

Supplies: Patterned paper (Sassafras Lass); chipboard bird (Maya Road); letters (Trends); decorative pins (Heidi Grace); brads, photo turns (Craft Affair); stickers (SRM Press); Misc: crepe paper, brown paper, thread, buttons, glitter mist, 3D dots, googly eye, Times New Roman font

Guitar

Amanda L. Torres
Spring Hill, FL

Supplies: Patterned paper, stickers (Sassafras Lass); letters (Sassafras Lass, American Crafts); Misc: pen

Barber Shop Duet

Keandra Perkins-Willis
New Orleans, LA

Supplies: Cardstock (Cardstock Warehouse, DCWV); patterned paper (Teresa Collins); watercolor paper (Canson); letters (Jenni Bowlin, Sassafras Lass); chipboard buttons (Jenni Bowlin); tags (Elle's Studio); chipboard sticker (BasicGrey); buttons (American Crafts); gaffer tape (7gypsies); dimensional paint (Ranger)

Rock Star

Dee Gallimore-Perry
Griswold, CT

Supplies: Cardstock (Core'dinations); patterned paper (My Mind's Eye, Sassafras Lass); letters (American Crafts, Doodlebug, Making Memories); embellishments (My Mind's Eye, BasicGrey, Fancy Pants, BoBunny); Misc: ink, punch, sewing machine, Wacky Action BTN font

Inspired Idea!

A good way to keep the page from getting too overwhelming is to convert your photos to black and white. Leaving just one solid-colored element on one photo (like the red guitar here) adds an artistic flair to an artistic page.

Rocker

Stephanie Hunn
Aurora, CO

Supplies: Patterned paper, stickers, transparency embellishments, journaling spot, fabric tag (Little Yellow Bicycle); letters (American Crafts)

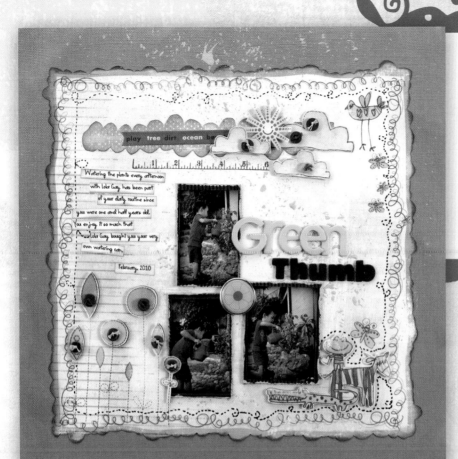

Green Thumb

Helga Payawal-Vergara
Masaya Bay, Laguna, Philippines

Supplies: Cardstock (Bazzill); patterned paper (Prima, Cosmo Cricket); letters (Fynmark, All About Scrapbooking); ribbon (KI Memories); brads (Kaisercraft); stamp (Technique Tuesday); Misc: glaze pen, acrylic paint, floss, buttons

He Gardens

Jing-Jing Nickel
Roseville, MN

Supplies: Cardstock (Bazzill); patterned paper, chipboard (Crate Paper); letters (Jillibean Soup, October Afternoon); Misc: punch, Underwood Champion font

The Fruits of His Labor

Connie Hyde Mercer
Belmont, TX

Supplies: Cardstock (Bazzill); patterned paper (BasicGrey); journal paper, chipboard (Jenni Bowlin); letters (American Crafts, Making Memories); flowers (Prima); pearls (Kaisercraft); Misc: baker's twine, border punch, button

Inspired Idea!

If the patterns on your patterned paper catch your eye but prove a little too large for the layout you're designing, consider hand-cutting it away from the background and using it as an embellishment. These large flowers, cut from patterned paper, create a dramatic effect. Instead of getting lost in the background, they become leading players.

How Does Ur Garden Grow?

Ria Mojica
Pasig, Metro Manila, Philippines

Supplies: Cardstock (Bazzill, DCWV, KI Memories); patterned paper (Tinkering Ink); die-cut paper (Creative Imaginations); letters (American Crafts); Misc: ink, pen, label maker

Chapter Two:

FUN TIMES

We scrapbook for so many different reasons.

We document birthdays, anniversaries, milestones—
we may even create as a form of therapy—but one of
the best reasons to scrapbook is just for the fun of it!
Of course you'll have fun when you sit down to
create your next masterpiece, but you can double the
enjoyment by scrapbooking all the fun things you do
every day!

From the special vacations you take together as a
family to the annual fall trip to the pumpkin patch,
you're making memories that last a lifetime. You don't
want to forget that trip to the zoo, the first roller coast-
er ride of the summer or the sports you participate
in every year! These fun times offer some of the best
memories...and your best memories deserve
to be scrapped!

kids needed to take
a break from long
hikes & riding in
van for sight seeing and

shopping from
time to time during
our trips. So, we let kids
to swim and get wet!

Inspired Idea!

Adding paint to your scrapbook layouts is a fun way to get artsy—and you don't have to relegate your artistic attempts to traditional methods! Paintbrushes make great applicators, to be sure, but don't stop there. Try Q-tips, bubble wrap, tinfoil, even a toothpick—like Bonnie did here for her tiny white dots and her journaling guidelines. Have fun discovering new results with every try!

Get Wet

Bonnie Fechter
Wyoming, MN

Supplies: Cardstock (KI Memories); patterned paper (Autumn Leaves, Chatterbox); letters (Making Memories, Doodlebug); punch (Fiskars); tag (Heidi Swapp); Misc: felt, thread, acrylic paint, rhinestone stickers, pen, adhesive foam squares

Inspired Idea!

You may find that your photos and journaling don't leave much room for the pretty embellishments you've been saving in your stash! No problem—cluster several small embellishments together around the key elements like the title, photos and journaling for tiny tidbits that pack a powerful punch.

A Whale of a Good Time

Robin Cuevas
Jacksonville, FL

Supplies: Cardstock (Bazzill); patterned paper; stickers (K&Co); letters (K&Co, Making Memories); felt (Making Memories); paper trim, brads (Doodlebug); flowers (Prima); buttons (Fancy Pants); Misc: pen, glitter mist

Slide Ride Denied

Andrea Friebus
La Habra, CA

Supplies: Cardstock (Bazzill, Stampin' Up); patterned paper (Provo Craft, Fancy Pants, Heidi Swapp); die-cuts (Scenic Route); brads (Making Memories); stickers (K&Co); plastic file tabs (Heidi Swapp); photo turn (Oriental Trading Company); Misc: ink, tickets, Arial font

slide ride DENIED

euroslide.com

Ready
UHH YEA RIGHT
SET
STRAIGHT TO THE POINT
WHO KNEW
GO
LOW IMPACT
GO EVERYWHERE
EXTREME
drama

Seeing this 2 year old screaming his head off going down these slides at the fair, you'd think he was terrified. Not so with our little guy. Turns out he wasn't scared at all—the screaming was him throwing a fit because he wanted to go down the blue slide, not the orange one.

time to meet SpONgebOb

SpongeBob

Ali Lacher
Bloomington, MN

Supplies: Cardstock (Bazzill); patterned paper (unknown); letters (QuicKutz, Doodlebug)

Ben and Alexa meeting Spongebob at Nickelodeon Universe Summer 2009

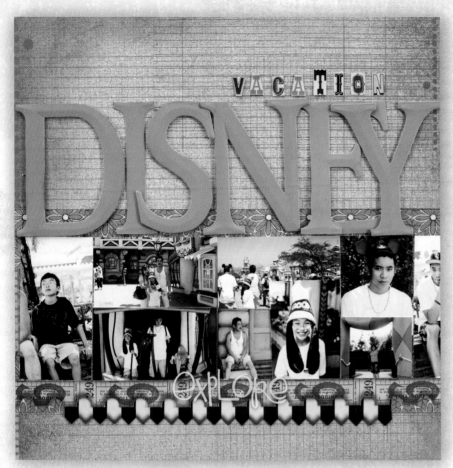

Disney Vacation

Juliet Adora Concepcion
Renton, WA

Supplies: Patterned paper (BasicGrey, Sassafras Lass); letters (SEI); sticker (Heidi Swapp)

Swinger!

Lisa Hoel
San Jose, CA

Supplies: Patterned paper (Fancy Pants, Scenic Route); letters (American Crafts); grungeboard wings (Advantus); acrylic stamps (Close To My Heart); glitter glue (Ranger); Misc: pen, ink, acrylic paint, punches, chipboard bracket, embossing powder

Inspired Idea!

Scrapbookers are notorious pack rats, so chances are you have a sheet of patterned paper with designs you've cut away to use in a layout. What do you do with the sheet that's left? Why not layer another pattern behind the cutaway elements for an entirely new look, giving them a second chance to pop off a page? Embellish the new design any way you please—it's sure to stand out as something special.

Children's Museum

Pamela Young
Thornton, CO

Supplies: Patterned paper, flower, gems (Prima); journaling spot (Jenni Bowlin); twill (DCWV); letters (American Crafts); button (Rusty Pickle); Misc: floss

At The Zoo With Kangarooi

Ashley C. Riley
New Orleans, LA

Supplies: Cardstock (Bazzill); patterned paper (Scenic Route); stickers (Sassafras Lass); letters (Making Memories, American Crafts); brads (Sassafras Lass); die-cuts, adhesive trim (K&Co); stamp (Studio Calico); leaf pins (Maya Road); felt leaf (Making Memories); Misc: pen, ink

Squeal

Michelle Houghton
Clive, IA

Supplies: Cardstock (Bazzill): sheer tag (Maya Road); letters (BasicGrey); brad (American Crafts); Misc: thread, pen, felt, rick rack

Well Hello There

Lisa VanderVeen
(Memory Makers Master, 2006)
Santa Monica, CA

Supplies: Software (Adobe Photoshop Elements 7); template (Jessica Sprague); patterned paper, stickers by Crystal Wilkerson (Jessica Sprague); Misc: staples

Spotlight On...

Becky Fleck
Columbus, MT

Becky Fleck
is the author of *Scrapbook PageMaps* and *Scrapbook PageMaps 2*. In the books, you'll see that whipping up a creative page design is a breeze with original sketches and amazing projects based on the sketches. Both books include take-along cards for scrapping on the go.

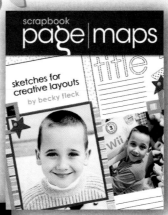

For You!
Supplies: Cardstock (BoBunny); patterned paper (BasicGrey, Crate Paper, Fancy Pants, My Mind's Eye); letters (BoBunny); brads (Imaginisce); crocheted flowers (Becky Fleck, pattern by Nichole Heady); stickers (BasicGrey, Cosmo Cricket)

Two Button Birdies

Supplies: Patterned paper (Pink Paislee); buttons (Fancy Pants); felt heart (BasicGrey); glitter (Pink Paislee); scallop paper punch (Martha Stewart Crafts); pen (EK Success); Misc: google eyes

She Loves The Fair

Jill Sarginson
Kanata, Ontario

Supplies: Patterned paper (Sassafras Lass); letters (Doodlebug, Sassafras Lass, Jenni Bowlin); stickers (Sassafras Lass); Misc: pen, buttons, floss, circle template, edge distresser, chipboard

Happiest Place On Earth

Virginia Wong
Calgary, Alberta

Supplies: Cardstock (Bazzill); patterned paper, letters, felt accents (Chatterbox); Misc: stitching

I don't know another kid that loves the park as much as you do! No matter how many times we go, it is a new and exciting experience – and you know what? I love that about you! I just adore our special park times!

Tractor!

Katie Saylor
San Antonio, TX

Supplies: Cardstock (Paper Studio); patterned paper (October Afternoon, Sassafras Lass); stickers (American Crafts); Misc: edge distresser, adhesive foam, embroidery floss

A Perfect Day

Tatum Woodroffe
Roxby Dawns, South Australia

Supplies: Patterned paper (Jillibean Soup, Jenni Bowlin, Rouge de Garance, Scenic Route, Sassafras Lass); stickers (Creative Imaginations, Jenni Bowlin); letters (American Crafts); journaling spots (Jillibean Soup); brads (Sassafras Lass, K&Co, Imaginesce); flowers (Prima, American Crafts); Misc: string, fabric

My Little Supergirl

Becky Williams
Wolfforth, TX

Supplies: Cardstock (Kraft); patterned paper (October Afternoon, Jillibean Soup), stickers (American Crafts, Sassafras Lass), journal spot (October Afternoon), frame (Making Memories), pearl (Kaisercraft), rub-ons (October Afternoon), felt star (Fancy Pants)

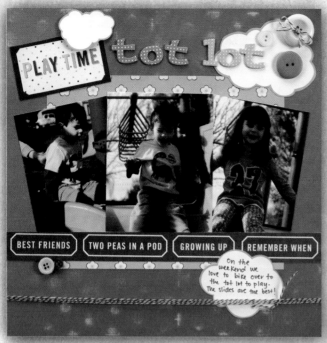

Tot Lot

Rebecca Keppel
Gilbert, AZ

Cardstock (Core'dinations); patterned paper (Cosmo Cricket, American Crafts); letters (American Crafts); buttons (Cosmo Cricket); baker's twine (Martha Stewart Crafts); Misc: pen

Explore

Guiseppa Gubler
Wellsville, UT

Supplies: Cardstock (Bazzill); patterned paper, letters (Bella Blvd); photo corner (Making Memories); brad (SEI); adhesive foam (All Night Media); acrylic star (Heidi Swapp); Misc: Lucinda Bright font

Whee!

Katie Saylor
San Antonio, TX

Supplies: Cardstock (BoBunny); patterned paper (BasicGrey, October Afternoon, Sassafras Lass); stickers (American Crafts); Misc: adhesive foam, Segoe Print font

Faster Daddy

Brianne Nevill
Fort Lewis, WA

Supplies: Cardstock (Bazzill); patterned paper (Glitz); letters (American Crafts, Doodlebug, Making Memories); felt (Fancy Pants); chipboard (Cosmo Cricket); badges, brads (American Crafts)

Inspired Idea!

You captured that special moment, but the photos are all blurry. Instead of getting upset and enrolling in a photography class, consider the alternative—scrapping it anyway! Documenting the memory—even in an imperfect photo—is better than not documenting it at all. Cut yourself some slack and enjoy the end result: a layout your family will treasure.

Flying

Michelle Houghton
Clive, IA

Supplies: Cardstock (American Crafts); patterned paper (Scenic Route); buttons (Paper Studio); rhinestones (Darice); letters (Creative Cafe); fabric leaf (Creative Impressions); Misc: pen, floss, rick rack

Biker Dude

Connie Hyde Mercer
Belmont, TX

Supplies: Cardstock (Bazzill); patterned paper (Sassafras Lass); trim (Wrights); letters (American Crafts, Making Memories); stickers (Sassafras Lass); ticket (Jenni Bowlin); Misc: pen, buttons, border punch, ink

Ride

Melanie Smith
Conception Bay South, Newfoundland

Supplies: Cardstock (Bazzill); patterned paper (American Crafts); letters (Heidi Swapp); Misc: chipboard, rub-ons

Scooter Gal

Wendy Kwok
Singapore

Supplies: Patterned paper (Pink Paislee); letters (American Crafts)

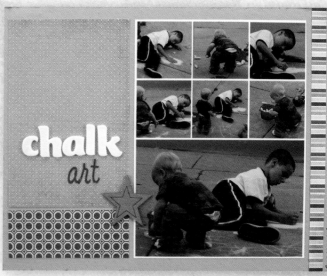

Chalk Art

Jessica Jo Salber
Wausau, WI

Supplies: Cardstock (The Paper Company); patterned paper (BasicGrey); chipboard stars (Magistical Memories); letters (American Crafts, BasicGrey); Misc: pen, ink

Dude!

Lydia Wiley
Ozawkie, KS

Supplies: Cardstock (DCWV); patterned paper, tags, letters, trim (Making Memories); Misc: brad, pen, ink

Extra! Extra!
ONE SKETCH, THREE WAYS

These three layouts, all based on this sketch, show you how take a sketch and stretch your inspiration to create multiple pages.

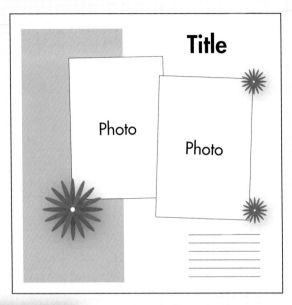

Swing

Michelle Houghton
Clive, IA

Supplies: Cardstock (American Crafts); patterned paper, chipboard elements, stickers (Sassafras Lass); rhinestones (Darice); buttons (Paper Studio); Misc: pen, floss, ribbon

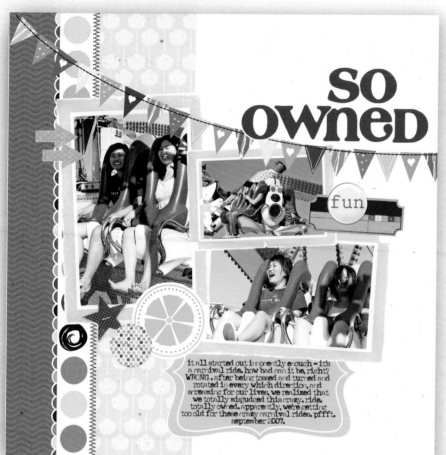

So Owned

Caroline Ikeji
(Memory Makers Master, 2008)

San Francisco, CA

Supplies: Software (Adobe Photoshop CS3); paper by Betsy Tuma; paper, border, pennant banners, ticket by Vinnie Pearce; arrows, dotted circle, star, flower circle, journaling tag, letters by Crystal Wilkerson; epoxy accent by Kate Teague; stitching by Tia Bennett; frame by Brandy Buffington (all digital elements from Two Peas in a Bucket); Misc: AL Modern Type font

Bowl of Cherries

Tracie Radtke
(Memory Makers Master, 2008)
Chicago, IL

Supplies: All supplies by Emily Powers (Oscraps); Misc: Century Gothic font, AL Professor font

Play

Muriel Croom
Chula Vista, CA

Supplies: Patterned paper (Sassafras Lass); letters (American Crafts); buttons (SEI); sticker (Making Memories); Misc: pen

Playtime

Katharyn Brine
Murrumbateman, Australia

Supplies: Software (Adobe Photoshop Elements 6); cardstock (Peppermint Creative, Shabby Miss Jenn); patterned paper (Ali Edwards); journaling spot (Cen's Loft); fabric (Lindsay Jane); stickers (Designer Digitals, CatScrap); pegs, painted splashes (Designer Digitals); Misc: Papyrus font

Playtime

Vicki Flinchum
Round Rock, TX

Supplies: Patterned paper, bling, letters (Prima); brads, photo turns (Queen & Co, Making Memories); laminating sheet, laminator, trimmer, decorative blades (Purple Cows); software (Adobe Photoshop Elements 2.0); acrylic paint (Ranger); alcohol ink (Ranger); embroidery floss (DMC); markers (Copic); Misc: crinoline, cardboard package insert

Girls' Day Out

Melanie Smith
Conception Bay South, Newfoundland

Supplies: Patterned paper (Scenic Route, October Afternoon, BasicGrey); letters (Scenic Route); Misc: acetate

Red, White & Blew

Andrea Friebus
La Habra, CA

Supplies: Cardstock (Bazzill, Stampin' Up!); patterned paper (Scenic Route); jewels (Prima); stickers (Making Memories, 7gypsies); rub-on transfers (Autumn Leaves, Hambly); brads (Making Memories); photo turns (Oriental Trading Company); felt (Creative Imaginations); plastic tags (Around the Block); die-cut machine (Making Memories); adhesive (Therm O Web); Misc: ink, pen, photo corners, ribbon, bookplate

Duplo Building

Natalija Elijas
Backi Petrovac, Serbia

Supplies: Software (Adobe Photoshop CS2); basic black paper, trim, doodles (Wackadoo); elements (Digital Scrapbook Place); Misc: Orator Std font, DSP Abby font

Loves 2 Paint

Lynn Y. Kopas
North Attleboro, MA

Supplies: Cardstock (BoBunny); patterned paper (October Afternoon, Sassafras Lass); letters (BasicGrey, Making Memories); journaling card (October Afternoon); cardstock stickers (Sassafras Lass); die-cut "Fig" stickers (Daisy D's); acrylic paint (Making Memories); ink (Colorbök); Misc: Prima Pebbles, buttons, baker's twine, floss, jute, staples, splat brad, tiny office clips, tickets, corrugated cardboard, paintbrush tip, black marker, adhesive foam

Another Epic Game

Terri Hayes
Cary, NC

Supplies: Cardstock (Prism); patterned paper, buttons (Sassafras Lass); trim (Webster's Pages); stickers (7gypsies, Creative Café, Luxe, Making Memories, My Little Shoebox, Pink Paislee); chipboard (Scenic Route); transparency (My Mind's Eye), die-cut (My Mind's Eye); Misc: pen

Inspired Idea!

It happens to all of us. We need a letter "E" and we've already used up every one that came in the package. When it comes to chipboard, using the negative space is not only cost effective, but it's visually appealing as well! The title on this layout would look fine if the "E" looked like all the other letters, but using the negative space makes it pop!

Games

Pamela Young
Thornton, CO

Supplies: Cardstock (American Crafts); patterned paper, die-cuts, letters (My Little Shoebox); Misc: glitter pen

The Gamer

Bonnie Fechter
Wyoming, MN

Supplies: Cardstock (KI Memories); patterned paper (Around the Block); letters (Doodlebug); circle cutter (Creative Memories); Misc: pen, brads

Water Fun

Denise C. Lofts
Lenexa, KS

Supplies: Cardstock (Bazzill); patterned paper (Quick Quotes); letters (American Crafts); journaling tags (Pink Paislee); epoxy buttons (Making Memories); stickers (Martha Stewart Crafts)

Inspired Idea!

Sometimes when looking at a blank 12" × 12" sheet of cardstock, we can feel the need to fill every square inch of the space, but the fact is that leaving white space on your layout can be an equally strong design choice. The absence of "stuff" on a layout creates a clean aesthetic and gives the eye a place to rest. Try using only a portion of your background and admire how clean your finished layout looks!

Oops!

Janine Worthington
Whangarei, New Zealand

Supplies: Cardstock (Bazzill); patterned paper (BasicGrey); transparencies (Autumn Leaves, Hambly); embellishments (7gypsies, Maya Road, Tanya Leigh Designs); Misc: pen, staples

Raingutter Regatta

Amy Wheeler
Cecilia, KY

Supplies: Cardstock (American Crafts); patterned paper (October Afternoon, Jenni Bowlin); journal card (Jenni Bowlin); letters (Jenni Bowlin, American Crafts); stickers (October Afternoon); film strip ribbon (Tim Holtz); Misc: pen, adhesive foam

Joy of Learning

Serena Gedlaman
Calgary, Alberta

Supplies: Patterned paper (Cosmo Cricket, We R Memory Keepers); buttons (BasicGrey, Daisy D's, Making Memories); metal (Making Memories); stickers (Cloud 9); letters (Cosmo Cricket); ribbon (Making Memories); Misc: pen, edge punch, ink

Aqua Kids

Jessica Jo Salber
Wausau, WI

Supplies: Cardstock (The Paper Company); patterned paper (Jillibean Soup); letters (Bella Blvd., BasicGrey); border punch (Fiskars); Misc: ink, pen, thread, buttons, brads

High Noon

Dora Phillips
Lisle, IL

Supplies: Patterned paper (Crate Paper); die-cuts (GCD Studios, My Mind's Eye); letters (American Crafts); bling (Kaisercraft); badge, stickers (American Crafts); punches (Fiskars); software (Adobe); Misc: sewing machine, thread, Mom's Hand font

Water Fight

Meg Barker
Detroit Lakes, MN

Supplies: Patterned paper (Bazzill, My Mind's Eye); letters (Doodlebug, Heidi Grace); trims (Heidi Grace, Li'l Davis); Misc: pen, staples

He Loves Water

Lynn Y. Kopas
North Attleboro, MA

Supplies: Patterned paper, die-cuts (BasicGrey); letters (Making Memories, BasicGrey); punch (EK Success); ink (Colorbök); tickets (Jenni Bowlin); Misc: jute, staples, brads, brown pen, stick pins, corrugated cardboard, adhesive foam tape

Love To Fish

Beth Price
Westfield, IN

Supplies: Cardstock (DCWV, Bazzill); patterned paper (Prima); letters (October Afternoon, KI Memories); glitter (Ranger); ink (Stampin' Up); Misc: gel pen, black embroidery floss

Boatload of Fun

Laina Lamb
Bay Village, OH

Supplies: Cardstock (Archiver's, Bazzill); patterned paper (Imaginisce, Scenic Route, BoBunny, KI Memories, October Afternoon); stickers (Sassafras Lass); letters (American Crafts, BasicGrey); ribbon (Cosmo Cricket); epoxy accent (KI Memories)

7K

Hera Frei
Kusnacht, Switzerland

Supplies: Cardstock (Core'dinations); patterned paper, stickers (October Afternoon); letters (American Crafts); buttons (BasicGrey); punch (Creative Memories, EK Success); Misc: Artisan font

Sunday Afternoon

Rosalie Vos Tulp
Ames, IA

Supplies: Software (Adobe Photoshop Elements 6.0); template (Senovia Designs); paper, page elements (Go Digital); Misc: Century Gothic font, Rage Italic font

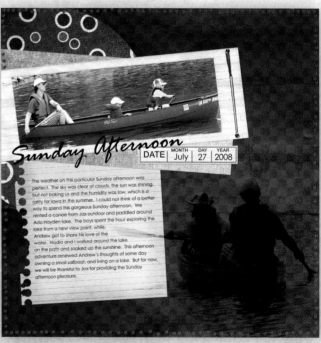

Camera Queen

Bethany Kartchner
Laveen, AZ

Supplies: Cardstock (Bazzill); patterned paper (Harmonie); frame (Sassafras Lass); chipboard bird (American Crafts); stamps (Hero Arts, Stampotique, Heidi Swapp); letters, overlay clouds (My Little Shoebox); flower (Prima); acrylic paint (Shimmerz); Misc: ink, pen, transparency, scissors, bling

Leamington Marina

Monique McCarthy
Ruthven, Ontario

*Supplies: Cardstock, ink (Close To My Heart); patterned paper, buttons (Cosmo Cricket); license plate (Karen Foster);
Misc: pen, adhesive, silver brads, twine*

Water Happies

Amy Martin
(Memory Makers Master 2009)
Corpus Christi, TX

*Supplies: Software (Corel PaintShopPro);
letters (Little Dreamer Designs); border
(Crate Paper); frame (Sassafras Lass);
Misc: Kenner Road kit, Last Words font*

Sandbox

Stacy Cohen
Los Angeles, CA

Supplies: Cardstock (Bazzill); patterned paper (Graphic 45); flowers (Prima); frame (Maya Road); rhinestone brad (Little Yellow Bicycle); Misc: embroidery thread, acrylic paint, glitter, Scrabble tiles

Lake Lovers

Keandra Perkins-Willis
New Orleans, LA

Supplies: Cardstock (Bazzill); patterned paper (Sassafras Lass); corrugated letters (Rusty Pickle, American Crafts); rub-ons (Daisy D's); eyelets (Making Memories); Misc: baker's twine, floss

Out To "Sea" a Shark

Sarah de Guzman
Sunnyvale, CA

Supplies: Cardstock (DCWV); patterned paper (Kiki Art, Sassafras Lass); letters (Sassafras Lass); Misc: adhesive foam

Cape Mermaid

Bethany Kartchner
Laveen, AZ

Supplies: Cardstock (Bazzill); patterned paper, ribbon (Harmonie); letters (American Crafts); chipboard circle element (Sassafras Lass); bling (Prima); scallop border (GCD Studios); stamps (Hero Arts, JudiKins); spritz, acrylic paint (Shimmerz); mask (Heidi Swapp); Misc: pen, scissors, thread, sewing machine, ink

Dirt

Gretchen McElveen
(Memory Makers Master, 2009)
Helena, AL

Supplies: Patterned paper, letters (Jillibean Soup); brads (American Crafts); journaling spot (Jenni Bowlin); ribbon (Three Bugs in a Rug); Misc: pen, corner rounder

Got Dirt?

Jackie Weeks
Fort Pierce, FL

Supplies: Cardstock (Bazzill); patterned paper, stickers (Adornit); letters (American Crafts); glitter mist (Tattered Angels); Misc: ink, twine, cardboard

Boys Will Be Boys

Katharyn Brine
Murrumbateman, Australia

Supplies: Software (Adobe Photoshop Elements 6); cardstock, patterned paper, WordArt (Kaisercraft); letters (Designer Digitals); punched date strip (Oscraps); Misc: Ali's font

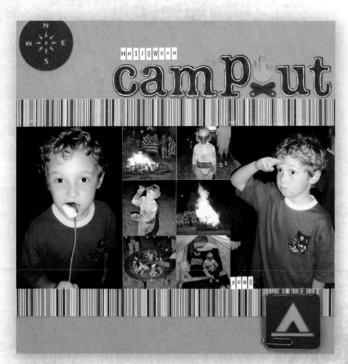

Halloween Campout

Ashley C. Riley
New Orleans, LA

Supplies: Cardstock (Bazzill); patterned paper (October Afternoon); letters (Sassafras Lass, Making Memories); die-cuts (Provo Craft); Misc: paper clip, staples

Happy Campers

Amanda L. Torres
Spring Hill, FL

Supplies: Cardstock (Bazzill); patterned paper (Three Bugs in a Rug, Crate Paper); chipboard (Maya Road, Crate Paper); stickers, brads (Crate Paper); letters (American Crafts); Misc: pen, glitter mist, ink

Mini Rock Climbing

Chrys Q. Rose
Tracy, CA

Supplies: Patterned paper, chipboard (Making Memories); stickers (Pink Paislee, Imagination Project)

Spotlight On...

Greta Hammond
Wakarusa, IN

Greta Hammond
is the co-author of *Kick It Up!*. Each idea presented in *Kick It Up!* is accompanied by two layouts: one that shows a well-designed page and a second that shows the same layout kicked up to the next level. The techniques range from the simple to the more advanced, and the visual evidence shows you exactly what it takes to spice up a layout.

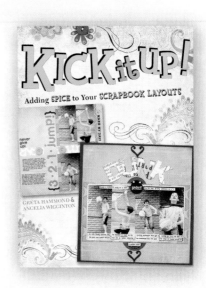

Surfer Girl

Supplies: Cardstock (WorldWin); patterned and die-cut paper, die-cut border, letters, epoxy stickers, gems (Little Yellow Bicycle); letters (BasicGrey); chipboard flower (Fancy Pants); Misc: Calibri font

Xtreme Chess, Anyone?

Supplies: Patterned paper, photo frame, dimensional sticker, letters, metal accents (Little Yellow Bicycle); letters (BasicGrey); Misc: Calibri font

Snow Tubing

Dawne Ivey
Cantonment, FL

Supplies: Patterned paper, rub-ons (Pink Paislee); letters (American Crafts, October Afternoon); border punch (Martha Stewart Crafts); floss (DMC)

Who Knew?

Ann Schneider
Rochester, NY

Supplies: Cardstock (The Paper Company); patterned paper (K&Co, Sassafras, Bella Blvd); letters (American Crafts); stickers (October Afternoon, Making Memories); flowers (K&Co, Making Memories); tags, tickets (K&Co); journaling spot (unknown); Misc: pen

Inspired Idea!

When grouping embellishments, use odd numbers. The buttons on this layout are grouped in threes, making them more interesting than even-numbered groupings. The groups also form a visual triangle around the photos, moving the eye exactly where it needs to go!

Sledding Fun

Rosalie Vos Tulp
Ames, IA

Supplies: Patterned paper (Studio Calico, BasicGrey); letters (American Crafts); buttons (BasicGrey); rhinestones (Kaisercraft); scallop scissors (Fiskars); Misc: machine stitching, Tahoma font

Red Deer

Jolene Johnston
Fishers, IN

Supplies: Patterned paper, journaling tags, buttons (BasicGrey); stamps (myStamp BOX, Colorbök); Misc: twine, ink

Inspired Idea!

The photo placement is what makes this two-page layout so well designed. With the grouping of photos lined up right at the center, the two pages instantly become more cohesive. Rather than having various elements floating around the two sheets of cardstock, these photos hug the center, grounding the entire layout in an interesting and eye-pleasing way.

Our Farm

Brenda Johnston
Roseville, CA

Supplies: Cardstock (Bazzill); patterned paper (Jillibean Soup); letters (American Crafts, My Little Shoebox); Misc: pen

Pony Express

Andrea Friebus
La Habra, CA

Supplies: Cardstock (Bazzill); patterned paper (Cosmo Cricket, K&Co, Sassafras Lass); rub-on transfers (Autumn Leaves); brads (Doodlebug); stickers (Cosmo Cricket); die-cut machine (Making Memories); Misc: ink, pen

Hay There

Katie Saylor
San Antonio, TX

Supplies: Patterned paper (BasicGrey); letters (Making Memories); stickers (Sassafras Lass); grunge board (Tim Holtz); Misc: stamp, sewing machine, thread

Soccer Sweetie

Beth Hallgren
Hartford, MI

Supplies: Cardstock (DCWV, Bazzill); patterned paper (DCWV); buttons (BoBunny); flower sequins (K&Co); title (Provo Craft); sticker (Making Memories); glitter glue (Ranger); punches (Fiskars); Misc: brads, pen, glitter mist

Hole In One

Hilde Janbroers
Leidschendam, Zuid-Holland, Netherlands

Supplies: Patterned paper, trim (Webster's Pages); flowers (Prima); letters (Prima, Webster's Pages); brads (Nikki Sivils); pearl swirls (ZVA Creative)

Our Team

Heather Pittman
Salem, OH

Supplies: Patterned paper (Best Creation, BoBunny); cut-outs (BoBunny); bingo card (Jenni Bowlin); definition (Scrappin' Sports Stuff); brads (Around the Block, Karen Foster); stickles (Ranger); letters (American Crafts); Misc. pen, paper clip

Sprint Duathlon

Beth Sears
Quispamsis, British Columbia

Supplies: Cardstock (Bazzill); patterned paper (My Mind's Eye); letters (American Crafts, Pink Paislee, My Little Shoebox, Jenni Bowlin); die-cuts (My Mind's Eye); brads (American Crafts)

Inspired Idea!

Celebrate your accomplishments! Come on, you deserve it! You may spend most of your time scrapbooking stories about other people. You've got every award your kids have won marked and honored in paper and pictures! But what about you? Next time you do something brave, remarkable or just plain fun, take pictures and journal about the experience. Your scrapbooks aren't complete if you never make an appearance in them.

My First 5K

Melissa Thiede
Grand Rapids, MI

Supplies: Cardstock (Stampin' Up); patterned paper (It Takes Two); stickers (Making Memories); letters (QuicKutz); punch (EK Success, Stampin' Up); Misc: acrylic paint, Tangerine font, Moxie font, Mary Jane font

Inspired Idea!

Overlapping your photos is the best way to fit more of them on the page. Next time you want to cram a bunch together, look for the white space in the photos. Somebody's back, an open ice rink, the base of a tree—these things aren't essential and will give you a good spot to overlap a more meaningful photo.

Junior Jazz

Nicole Stark
(Memory Makers Master, 2007)
Roy, UT

Supplies: Cardstock (Bazzill); patterned paper (October Afternoon, American Crafts); tag (Creative Imaginations); stamp (Making Memories); die-cuts (Provo Craft); border punch (EK Success); chipboard (Jenni Bowlin, American Crafts); journaling spot (Jenni Bowlin); Misc: pen

Treat

Hera Frei
Kusnacht, Switzerland

Supplies: Patterned paper, ribbon, button (Jillibean Soup); letters (American Crafts, Jillibean Soup); punch (Creative Memories); Misc: string, Bernhard MT Condensed font

Keep Your Eyes On The Ball

Stacy Cohen
Los Angeles, CA

Supplies. Cardstock (Bazzill); patterned paper (Autumn Leaves); letters (Heidi Swapp, Pressed Petals); snaps (Making Memories); buttons (Favorite Findings); Misc: thread, pearls

You're A natural born athlete. One thing you love to do is play baseball with Daddy. Daddy taught you three things: keep your shoulders square, keep your elbows up, and keep your eyes on the ball!

The Wind Up

Amy Wheeler
Cecilia, KY

Supplies: Patterned paper (My Mind's Eye); letters (Making Memories, American Crafts); washers, snaps (Making Memories); Misc: pen, adhesive foam

He Loves to Play

Angela J. Prieto
Stockton, KS

Supplies: Patterned paper (We R Memory Keepers); rub-ons (Reminisce); letters (American Crafts); stickers (NRN Designs, MAMBI, Reminisce); gromlets (We R Memory Keepers); journaling card (Pebbles); Misc: pen

Inspired Idea!

Next time you want to really draw attention to a small part of your layout, pull out all the stops! This big, red arrow points directly to the ball in the focal point photo, making it impossible to ignore the baseball that's flying through the air. Chipboard or even hand-cut arrows would serve the same purpose and have the same effect.

Playing Ball

Julie K. Jundt
Owatonna, MN

Supplies: Software (Adobe Photoshop Elements); letters, digital elements, patterned paper, WordArt, journaling spot, frame, label, photo digital crop shape (Scrap Girls)

Thursday Getaway

Ann-Marie Morris
Simi Valley, CA

Supplies: Cardstock (Bazzill, DCWV); patterned paper (Cosmo Cricket, KI Memories); letters (BasicGrey); die-cut machine (Making Memories); ribbon (American Crafts); Misc: pens, punches, thread, staples

Date Night

Amanda L. Torres
Spring Hill, FL

Supplies: Cardstock (The Paper Company); patterned paper, stickers (Sassafras Lass); letters (Sassafras Lass, American Crafts); Misc: pen, glitter, ink

Sunday in San Francisco

Christyn Holmes
Littleton, CO

Supplies: Cardstock (Bazzill); patterned paper (Sassafras Lass, Making Memories); stickers (Sassafras Lass); letters (Cosmo Cricket, October Afternoon) Misc: ink, scalloped scissors, pen

Imagination

Star Rork
Saunemin, IL

Supplies: Cardstock (The Paper Studio); patterned paper (My Mind's Eye, October Afternoon); chipboard (Maya Road); ribbon (BasicGrey); Misc: cotton cord, ink, sewing, pen, border punch, scissors, trimmer

Harlem

Loredana Bucaria
Quarto Napoli, Italy

Supplies: Cardstock (Bazzill); patterned paper (American Crafts, BAM POP); stamps (October Afternoon, Studio Calico, Catslife Press, 7gypsies, American Crafts, Pink Paislee); stickers (7gypsies, Making Memories, American Crafts); brads (American Crafts); letters (American Crafts, Making Memories); embellishments (American Crafts, Tattered Angels); Misc: old book paper, masking tape, fabric, brown gel pen, pencil, brown ink, black ink

iPod Road Trip

Ashley C. Riley
New Orleans, LA

Supplies: Patterned paper, letters (Making Memories); fabric shape accent, foam shape stickers (American Crafts); Misc: label maker, chipboard

We saw Legally Blonde-the Musical. We went to the MARTHA STEWART SHOW, rode a carriage through CENTRAL PARK, and ate the best gnocchi @ BLT Market. We shopped @ Bergdorf Goodman's and had lunch @ BG-designed by Kelly Wearstler. We had the best seat in the house and tasty LOBSTER lasagna!

We also went to TIME SQUARE where we ate @ my new favorite restaurant-CARMINE'S twice. We had a drink @ the top of the Marriot-what a view!

Jina and I had such a great GIRLS' TRIP- lots of shopping, eating and WALKING! It was my first time in NEW YORK, and Jina was the best TOUR GUIDE!

Inspired Idea!

A great way to save space and still get a good amount of journaling on your layout is to cut thin strips. Simply type and print your journaling, then cut it out, layering it over the photos and other elements of your page. This makes the text less blocky and gives the page room to breathe, but doesn't sacrifice the whole story in the process.

2 Girls In The Big Apple

Ashley C. Riley
New Orleans, LA

Supplies: Cardstock (Bazzill); patterned paper (Making Memories, My Mind's Eye); letters (American Crafts, Making Memories); apple accent (October Afternoon); sticker label accents (Making Memories, Prima); brads (Making Memories); rub-ons (Marah Johnson); die-cuts (Provo Craft)

A View From Above

Julie Walton
Simi Valley, CA

Supplies: Software (Adobe); digital paper, digital elements (Pressed Petals); Misc: Wendy Medium font

Inspired Idea!

Fabric and canvas add such interesting detail to your scrapbook pages. By applying gesso and then paint to canvas and then cutting squares with pinking sheers, Wendi was able to create a unique embellishment to stitch to her layout. This instantly made the layout one of a kind. The addition of a hand-rolled flower embellishment finished the page off with gusto!

You Are Here

Wendi Manuel-Scott
Leesburg, VA

Supplies: Cardstock (American Crafts); patterned paper (Studio Calico, Crate Paper, BasicGrey, Cosmo Cricket); letters (Making Memories, BasicGrey); flowers (Sassafras Lass); labels (Studio Calico); journaling spots (Collage Press); acrylic paint (Maya Road); Misc: pen, punch

Explore

Romy Veul
Uithoorn, Netherlands

Supplies: Patterned paper, clear shapes (My Little Yellow Bicycle); crystal swirl, flowers (Prima); letters (American Crafts); buttons (BasicGrey); edge distresser (Heidi Swapp); liquid pearls (Ranger); Misc: black marker, white pen, punches, scissors, floss

Up Top

Davinie Fiero
Redmond, OR

Supplies: Cardstock (Bazzill, Kraft); patterned paper, yellow strip (Studio Calico); letters (Doodlebug); circle punch (Fiskars); Misc: buttons, machine stitching, Modern #20 font

May Flaum

is the coauthor of *Paper + Pixels*. Inside the book, discover the world of hybrid scrapbooking. Try 40 simple lessons that give you the how-to for using digital techniques that are as fun as using scissors and glue. Plus, the book includes a bonus CD with 10 exclusive scrapbook kits. Visit May at www.mayflaum.wordpress.com

Spotlight On...

May Flaum
Vacaville, CA

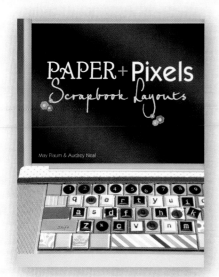

We love a good vacation, and what's not to love about a week long trip to Southern California? The time as a family, exploring places we'd only been previously in the time before kids, and enjoying all the sights, not to mention great meals made this trip memorable.

It's true that Elizabeth came down with the flu (H1N1) here, and that by the time we got home we all had it, but the memories up to that point were all wonderful, and the trip will be remembered fondly.

From the San Diego Zoo to eating at long time favorite restaurants, classic Disneyland rides to seeing Shamu, this was an amazing experience.

Vacation

Supplies: Patterned paper, artisan elements (Pink Paislee); digital papers by Lynn Grieveson (Designer Digitals); page template (Ali Edwards); flowers (Jillibean Soup); buttons (Jenni Bowlin); glitter mist (Tattered Angels); fabric strip (Studio Calico); Misc: rhinestones

Moments

Supplies: Cardstock (unknown); digital overlay (Ali Edwards); digital tickets (Rhonna Designs); digital star journaling, star accent by Katie Pertiet (Designer Digitals); felt accents (Valicious); border strip (GCD Studios); rhinestones (Kaisercraft); sticker (Bella Blvd); Misc: glitter, small buttons

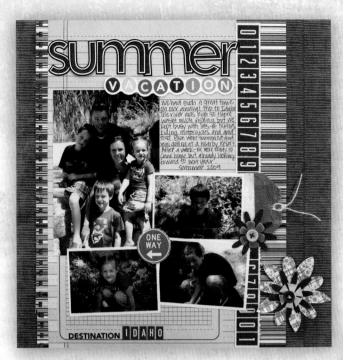

Summer Vacation

Brenda Hurd
Plain City, UT

*Supplies: Patterned paper (Studio Calico,
My Mind's Eye); die-cuts, letters (Sassafras
Lass, October Afternoon), Misc: pen, border
punch, floss*

Old Sac

Laura Achilles
Littleton, CO

*Supplies: Cardstock (Bazzill); patterned paper (7gyp-
sies, American Crafts, Jenni Bowlin); letters (American
Crafts, My Little Shoebox); chipboard frame (American
Crafts); stickers (7gypsies, Prima); rub-ons (Maya
Road); stamp (Kenner Road); glitter mist (Tattered
Angels); template (Crafter's Workshop);
Misc: ink, punch*

My Maine Squeeze

Lisa VanderVeen
(Memory Makers Master, 2006)
Santa Monica, CA

*Supplies: Software (Adobe Photoshop Elements 7); card
stock (My Own Creation); letters (Crystal Wilkerson); clip by
Katie Pertiet (Designer Digitals); heart pin by Leora (Designer
Digitals); frames (Carina Gardner, Rhonna Designs); overlays
(Carina Gardner); cardboard circle (Shawna Clingerman)*

The Mighty Colorado

Lisa VanderVeen
(Memory Makers Master, 2006)
Santa Monica, CA

Supplies: Software (Adobe Photoshop Elements 7); patterned paper, branch sticker, owl button by Jen Allyson (Two Peas in a Bucket); journaling stamps by Carina Gardner (Two Peas in a Bucket); stitching by Anna Aspnes (Designer Digitals)

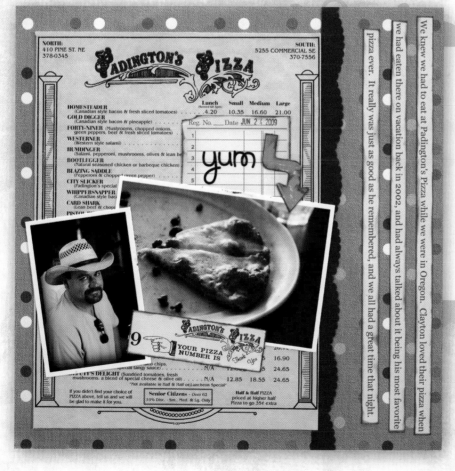

Inspired Idea!

We often save ticket stubs, receipts and other memorabilia from special occasions, but sometimes it's difficult to know what to do with them. Rather than stuffing them in a hidden pocket or envelope, try actually incorporating them into your layout as Mary Ann has done here with their order number and menu. These one-of-a-kind items instantly make the layout unique.

Vacation Pizza

Mary Ann Jenkins
Lakewood, CA

Supplies: Cardstock (Bazzill); patterned paper (DCWV); die-cut (Scenic Route); letters (KI Memories); Misc: menu, pizza claim number and order form, ink, punch

Amsterdam

Emeline Seet
Singapore

Supplies: Cardstock (Bazzill); patterned paper (The Girls' Paperie); stickers (7gypsies); chipboard (Maya Road); letters (Heidi Swapp); stamps (Purple Onion)

Rome

Meghann Andrew
New Orleans, LA

Supplies: Cardstock (Doodlebug, Bazzill); patterned paper (KI Memories, Cosmo Cricket, October Afternoon, Studio Calico); journaling circle (Elle's Studio); letters (American Crafts); flower (K&Co); key (7gypsies); rhinestone, brads, button (BasicGrey); metal clip (Making Memories); pearl (Kaisercraft); Misc: thread

Going to Rome for your birthday weekend was such a fantastic experience. Seeing the architectural sights, eating fantastic food & being immersed in the culture was amazing. August 09

The best part? Being there with you.

Red Square Day

Kathleen Summers
Roseville, CA

Supplies: Software (Adobe); cardstock, patterned paper, letters, buttons (Designer Digitals)

Inspired Idea!

How do you make a photo stand out on a page with lots of photos? Easy! Print two copies of the same photo. Position the first one on the page and then cut around the silhouette of the second one. Then, take the cut-out and apply it to the page with foam tape, making it instantly pop off the background in a cool and fun new way!

Kampong Holiday

Edleen Abdul
Singapore

Supplies: Patterned paper (Far Flung Craft, Sassafras Lass, Stemma); letters (American Crafts); rub-on (Kelly Panacci); sticker (Colorbök); stamps (Toga, Maya Road, Hero Arts, Heidi Swapp, Collage Press, Fontwerks); Misc: pen, dew drop, scissors, ink

Chapter Three:

HOLIDAYS, SEASONS AND SPECIAL OCCASIONS

It seems when we look back on our earliest memories, holidays and special events always appear to stand out. From hunting Easter eggs to decorating the Christmas tree, holidays are undoubtedly some of the most prominent memories in our lives. Special occasions offer memory landmarks as well, but scrapbooking birthdays, anniversaries and other annual events can get monotonous if you're not careful! This chapter provides tons of fabulous and fun ideas on keeping the pages that appear in your albums on a regular basis from becoming stale! If you're hoping to find new inspiration, you've certainly come to the right place. One look through this chapter and you'll emerge with many new ideas to make your holiday and special occasion pages shine!

Spring Has Sprung

Amanda L. Torres
Spring Hill, FL

Supplies: Cardstock (DCWV, The Paper Company); patterned paper, chipboard (American Crafts); letters (American Crafts, My Little Shoebox); Misc: pen, decorative scissors

Inspired Idea!

Who says toys are just for the kids? The flowers on this layout were created using a spirograph. The geometric drawing tool may not be your typical scrapbooking gizmo, but you can't argue with these kinds of results! What other fun toys do you have laying around your house that could create a unique addition to your next layout?

A Little Spring in Your Step

Andrea Freibus
In Habra, CA

Supplies: Cardstock, rub-ons (American Crafts); patterned paper (Provo Craft, Creative Memories, Heidi Grace); brads (Doodlebug, Queen & Co); buttons (Creative Imaginations); die-cut machine (Making Memories); adhesive (Therm O Web); Misc: pens, thread

Stop and Smell the Flowers

Stacy Cohen
Los Angeles, CA

Supplies: Cardstock (Bazzill); patterned paper (Graphic 45, Scenic Route); letters (BasicGrey); canvas (Ranger/Claudine Hellmuth); flowers (Prima); pearls (Kaisercraft); Misc: thread, Mod Podge, metal wire, gauze, ribbon

Really, Minnesota?!

Michele Skinner
Burnsville, MN

Supplies: Cardstock (Bazzill); patterned paper (BasicGrey, My Mind's Eye, SEI); die-cut paper (KI Memories); letters (American Crafts); letter stamps (Paper Source); Misc: adhesive, corner rounding punch, dimensional gloss medium, glitter, ink, pearls

Easter

Kristie Coleman
Franklin, TN

Supplies: Patterned paper (GCD Studios); letters (Pressed Petals); dimensional stickers (EK Success); Misc: beads, button, circle punch, eyelets, floss, ink, lace, ribbon, thread

Easter '09

Linda Sobolewski
Guilford, CT

Supplies: Cardstock (Bazzill); patterned paper (BasicGrey); die-cut eyelet paper, decorative pin, embroidery floss (Making Memories); journaling card, ribbon (Anna Griffin); fabric letters (American Crafts); buttons (Sassafras Lass); butterfly mini-stamp (Studio Calico); Misc: ink

Easter

Melanie Coombes
Snoqualmie, WA

Supplies: Patterned paper (CherryArte, DCWV, Hambly); letters (American Crafts); ribbon (DCWV); date stamp (Colop); Misc: pen, ribbon

The Eggs

Pamela Young
Thornton, CO

Supplies: Patterned paper, letters, lace (Rusty Pickle); pearls (Little Yellow Bicycle); Misc: sewing machine

Color Me Happy

Jill Paulson
Yankton, SD

Supplies: Cardstock (DCWV, Bazzill); patterned paper (Making Memories); Kraft paper (unknown); transparency (Prima); stickers, ribbon (Making Memories); letters (Doodlebug); brads (We R Memory Keepers); photo corner punch, pen (EK Success); Misc: staples

Inspired Idea!

Funky shapes make a layout so much more fun! Why not create shape templates for the shapes you use on a regular basis? Cut pre-sized photo templates, unique edged templates and anything else you can think of that may make a repeat appearance on your pages. You'll save yourself time and up your visual interest all at once!

A Day for the Dogs

Terri Hayes
Cary, NC

Supplies: Cardstock (Bazzill); patterned paper (Bella Blvd); stickers (Cosmo Cricket, Luxe, Scenic Route, Webster's Pages); transparency (My Mind's Eye), 3D embellishment (American Crafts); Misc: pen

Everyday Easter

Tiff Sawyer
Camden, Australia

Supplies: Cardstock (Making Memories); patterned paper (K&Co, Dream Street, Emily Falconbridge); chipboard flowers (BasicGrey); die-cut arrow (Scenic Route); letters (Pink Paislee, American Crafts); cardstock subtitles (My Mind's Eye); Misc: black felt pen

St. Patrick's Day Treasure

Andrea Friebus
La Habra, CA

Supplies: Cardstock (Bazzill); patterned paper (Sassafras Lass, Creative Memories, Daisy D's); stickers (My Little Shoebox); jewels (MAMBI); die-cut machine (Making Memories); adhesive (Therm O Web); Misc: ink, pen, punch

Mother's Day

Kathleen Summers
Roseville, CA

Supplies: Girlfriends kit: paper, stickers, green circle stitching, tag, paper buttons and letters (Julie Marie Designs); WordArt by Ali Edwards, white stitching by Anna Aspnes (Designer Digitals)

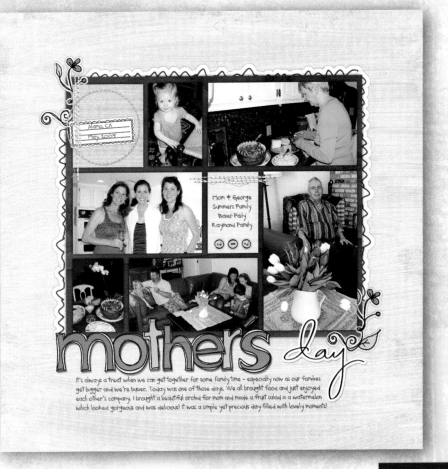

Spring Night

Lynn Warner
Coal Valley, IL

Supplies: Patterned paper, chipboard shapes, letters (Cosmo Cricket); pin (Maya Road); Misc: pen, ink, flower punch, vintage book page, vintage sheet music

Beaux Jours

Nathalie T. Arnulphy
Curepipe, Mauritius

Supplies: Cardstock (WorldWin); patterned paper (Cosmo Cricket); letters (Sizzix); Misc: acrylic paint, crackle accents, dymo, glitter, mounting tape, newspaper cuts, white pen

Spring is in the Air

Janine Buckles
London, Ontario

Supplies: Actions, letters, old chipboard letter templates, dynamic digital brush set, stitching, embellishments, digital papers (Scrap Girls); Misc: Calibri font

Inspired Idea!

Of course you have no problem overlapping your photos, but what about your embellishments? By placing a rub-on on top of alphabet stickers, you create a layered, well-designed title. This kind of layering automatically gives your page dimension and makes it more interesting to look at.

Summer Pool Party

Dee Gallimore-Perry
Griswold, CT

Supplies: Patterned papers (Scenic Route, October Afternoon); letters (American Crafts); acrylics, patch, epoxy sticker (KI Memories); die-cuts (October Afternoon, KI Memories, Making Memories); brads, chipboard, ribbon (BoBunny); rub-on (Scenic Route); paper border strips (Doodlebug); paper clip (KI Memories); Misc: Century Gothic font

Über Splash of Fun

Julie Overby
Waldport, OR

Supplies: Cardstock (Bazzill); patterned paper (GCD Studios); felt flowers, trim (Prima); stickers (American Crafts, Making Memories, Hambly); glitter mist (Tattered Angels); Misc: pens, ink

Saturday

Iara Gomes-Baer
Gummersbach, Germany

Supplies: Patterned paper (The Lilypad); background paper, label strip, journaler by Emily Powers (Oscraps); clear overlay, life preserver, felt frame (The Lilypad); frames by ON Designs (Scrapbook Graphics); stitches by Syrin (CatScrap)

Summer Fun

Kim Collee
Ridgeway, Ontario

Supplies: Cardstock (Bazzill); patterned paper, overlay (Fancy Pants); letters (Doodlebug); adhesive dots (3M)

everytime I turned around, Landon was COVERED

in sand. He had it everywhere!! In his hair, ears,

eyes, diapers!! He drove us crazy!!

But regardless Of what we felt, he was right at home in the sand!

The Sand Man

Kristin Hayne
Castle Rock, CO

Supplies: Cardstock (Bazzill); patterned paper, die-cut (Cosmo Cricket); letters (American Crafts, Pink Paislee); brads, shaped brads, felt shape (Queen & Co); acrylic paint (Making Memories); Misc: sand, pearl glaze, adhesive, CK Neat Freak font

So Hot

Liana Suwandi
Wylie, TX

Supplies: Cardstock (Bazzill); patterned paper, journal book, chipboard, ribbon, buttons (Fancy Pants); butterfly punch (Martha Stewart Crafts); brad (Queen & Co); jewel (EK Success); glitter rub-ons (We R Memory Keepers); hand-cut flower (from patterned paper by Fancy Pants); adhesive (Xyron); paper cutter (Purple Cows)

All Summer Long

Andrea Wiebe
Westbank, British Columbia

Supplies: Cardstock, patterned paper, ribbon (American Crafts); chipboard, wire flower (Maya Road); embroidery floss (DMC); letters (Cosmo Cricket); jewels (Prima); pen (Sharpie); Misc: cardboard, pearl gems, tag, ticket

Memories of Summer

Janis G. Medina-Maghinay
Makati City, Metro Manila,
Philippines

Supplies: Cardstock (Bazzill); patterned paper, chipboard shapes, stickers, letters (Bella Blvd); denim brackets (Buzz and Bloom); Misc: acrylic paint, bling, ink, pen, recycled chipboard frame

Yum

Janine Worthington
Whangarei, New Zealand

Supplies: Cardstock (Bazzill): patterned paper (BasicGrey); transparencies (Autumn Leaves, Hambly); embellishments (7gypsies, Maya Road, Tanya Leigh Designs); Misc: pen, staples

ON A HOT SUMMER DAY
YUMMY COOL ICECREAM
IS JUST THE BEST

life is good.

yum!

Ice cream after a
trip to the beach is a
summer tradition

Inspired Idea!

While scrapbooking is all about the photos, it's okay to highlight the products you love as well. If you are smitten with a certain patterned paper, simply print smaller photos, embellish them in one corner and add a few tidbits to tie it all together. By leaving patterned white space, your page is instantly decorated and instantly beautiful!

Sweet Treat

Kristy Dalman
Fennville, MI

Supplies: Cardstock (Bazzill); patterned paper, buttons (Sassafras Lass); letters (American Crafts, My Little Shoebox); digital stamp (Some Odd Girl); color spray (Tattered Angels); Misc: thread, pen, border punch, ink, marker

113

June Tradition

Jing-Jing Nickel
Roseville, MN

Supplies: Cardstock (Bazzill); patterned paper (October Afternoon); Plantin Schoolbook cartridge (Provo Craft); Misc: CK Footnote font

Juicy

Amy Martin
(Memory Makers Master, 2009)
Corpus Christi, TX

Supplies: Software (Corel PaintShopPro vXI); letters (Little Dreamer Designs); buttons (BasicGrey); stickers, paper (Sassafras Lass); Misc: embroidery floss, Kenner Road Kit, Maszyna Royal Dark font

Inspired Idea!

Linear pages are certainly clean and crisp, but a slightly tilted design shouldn't be underestimated. Mix it up a little by creating your next page at a slight angle—not so much that you have to tilt your head to look at it, but just enough to be interesting. That little change can go a long way.

Our Favorite Summer Spots

Nicole Carro
Stewartsville, NJ

Supplies: Cardstock (Bazzill); patterned paper (SEI, Chatterbox, BasicGrey, Prima); letters (Scrapworks); Misc: butterfly

Water Rockets

Stephenie Hamen
Sun Prairie, WI

Supplies: Cardstock (Bazzill); patterned paper (Cosmo Cricket); paper flowers (Prima); metal signs, frame (Making Memories, GCD Studios); calendar page, letters (Jenni Bowlin); trimmer, corner rounder, scallop punch (Fiskars); silver pen (Creative Memories); black pen (American Crafts); pearl bling (Kaisercraft); tulle and fabric flowers (handmade); Misc: adhesive foam, ribbon, fabric

Poppers

Grace Tolman
Garden Grove, CA

Supplies: Cardstock (Bazzill, The Paper Company); patterned paper, fabric brads (Upsy Daisy); letters (BasicGrey); glitter glue (Ranger); border punch (Fiskars); adhesive badge (Flair, American Crafts); ribbon (GCD Studios)

July 4th

Melanie Coombes
Snoqualmie, WA

Supplies: Cardstock (Bazzill); patterned paper (My Mind's Eye, Prima, Sassafras Lass); chipboard (DCWV); die-cut title (Crafty Secrets); Misc: buttons, ribbon, staples, Times New Roman font

July 4th

Lisa Hoel
San Jose, CA

Supplies: Metallic cardstock (unknown); patterned paper (Rusty Pickle); woven labels (Scrapworks); acrylic stamp (Autumn Leaves); Misc: pen, punch, glitter glue, bottle cap, chipboard shapes, thread, ink

Solemn Family Fourth

Keandra Perkins-Willis
New Orleans, LA

Supplies: Cardstock (Papertrey); patterned paper (American Crafts); stickers (Heidi Swapp, Making Memories); letters (Scenic Route); brads, eyelets (Making Memories); watercolor firecrackers and stars (Kiwi the Creator); spray mist (Tattered Angels); Misc: painter's tape floss

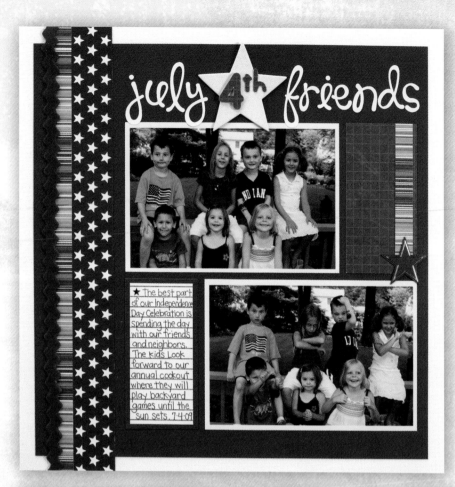

July 4th Friends

Laina Lamb
Bay Village, OH

Supplies: Cardstock (Bazzill); patterned paper (Scenic Route, Creative Imaginations, CherryArte); ribbon (May Arts); chipboard (3Birds); letters (Doodlebug); stickers (Stampendous)

Celebrate

Suzanna Lee
Glen Allen, VA

Supplies: Patterned paper (Creative Imaginations, Paper Adventures, Daisy D's, Rusty Pickle); journal spot (Making Memories); die-cuts (My Mind's Eye); stickers (Creative Imaginations); stamps (Autumn Leaves); ribbon (Making Memories); distresser (Tim Holtz); Misc: ink, liquid appliqué, punch

Inspired Idea!

It's tempting to trash those pesky scraps when you finish a page, but not so fast! Before you ditch the tiny bits of paper and ribbon you have left over, see if you can use them to create a completely new layout! Layering a variety of patterns together can create a lovely and interesting background. A few extra embellishments and you've got a page that came together in a snap!

I Love a Parade

Terri Hayes
Cary, NC

Supplies: Patterned paper (Dream Street, Graphic 45, Making Memories, MAMBI, October Afternoon, Pink Paislee, Webster's Pages); stickers, trim (Webster's Pages); chipboard (BasicGrey, Scenic Route); felt (Creative Imaginations, Jenni Bowlin, Queen & Co); crystals (Mark Richards); Misc: pen

Labor Day Fun

Linda Sobolewski
Guilford, CT

Supplies: Patterned paper (Sassafras Lass, BasicGrey); stickers (Sassafras Lass); letters, felt flower, button (BasicGrey); journaling piece (Little Yellow Bicycle); trim (Anna Griffin); labels (Jenni Bowlin); scrapper's floss (Karen Foster); Misc: punch

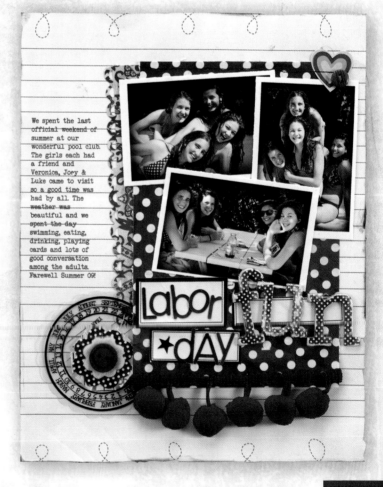

1st Day of 3rd Grade

Jessica Jo Salber
Wausau, WI

Supplies: Cardstock (Bazzill); patterned paper (Cosmo Cricket, American Crafts, October Afternoon); letters (American Crafts, Jenni Bowlin); journaling spot (October Afternoon); Misc: buttons, brads, ink

Off to School

Kristie Coleman
Franklin, TN

Supplies: Patterned paper, letters (Jillibean Soup); mini-letters (October Afternoon); Misc: thread, twine, punches, button, date stamp, tag, ink, pencil

Loving Fall

Melanie Smith
Conception Bay South, Newfoundland

Supplies: Patterned paper (BasicGrey, Making Memories, Cosmo Cricket); letters, buttons (Making Memories); flowers (BoBunny)

Leaf Collector

Heather Bowser
Brandon, MS

Supplies: Cardstock (Core'dinations); patterned paper (Cosmo Cricket); die-cut machine (Silhouette); Misc: vellum

While we were on a picnic in the fall,

Luke, you were so amazed at the colors of the leaves.

You collected a bunch and brought them home.

Nov 2009

Extra! Extra!

DIGITAL · HYBRID · TRADITIONAL

These layouts show how you can get inspired by a digital layout even if you're not a digital scrapper. The two layouts on the next page—one hybrid and one traditional—were both inspired by the digital layout below.

Puddle Jumper

Shannnon Trombley
Theresa, NY

Supplies: Software (Adobe Photoshop Elements 7.0); digital papers, embellishments, WordArt from Rain Rain Collection by Emily Card and Krystal Hartley (Scrap Orchard)

XOXOXO

Amy Martin
(Memory Makers Master, 2009)
Corpus Christi, TX

Supplies: Paper (Kenner Road,
Crate Paper, Jenni Bowlin); flower
(Amy Butler); acrylic paint (The
Lilypad); ribbon (May Arts); tag
(Fancy Pants); WordArt (Oscraps);
Misc: Maszyna Royal Light font

Winter Sweater

Melissa Blair
(Memory Makers Master, 2009)
Dover, AR

Supplies: Patterned paper
(BasicGrey, The Paper Studio);
adhesive dots (Therm O Web);
brads (Doodlebug); flowers
(Prima); stickers (BasicGrey, Cosmo
Cricket); punch (Fiskars)

An unexpected bonus of our new house is the glorious red foliage of the maple tree in our front yard. The red leaves get compliments from our neighbors and even Sofi's classmates. The leaves collect on top of my car and cling there during the drive to pre-school. On this fall day strong winds blew many of the leaves to the ground. They were the perfect playthings for Sofi. 10.30.2009

Maple Tree

Cathy Pascual
Bellevue, WA

Supplies: Software (Adobe); digital paper, blue tag, tree by Nancy Kubo (Little Dreamer Designs); green paper, doodled border, words by Crystal Wilkerson (Jessica Sprague); Misc: Harting font

Leaves and Me

Sarah de Guzman
Sunnyvale, CA

Supplies: Cardstock (Bazzill); patterned paper (Reminisce, Sassafras Lass); corrugated cardboard (Zutter); letters (Sassafras Lass); pearls (Queen and Co); punch (Imaginisce); Misc: brads, pen

Colors of Autumn

Muriel Croom
Chula Vista, CA

Supplies: Cardstock (Bazzill); patterned paper (Daisy D's, Pink Paislee); sticker (Daisy D's); stamp (Hampton Arts), vintage findings (Making Memories); digital frame by Sande Krieger (Two Peas in a Bucket); Misc: pen, copy paper, ink, binder clip, ticket

Garritys

Jill Paulson
Yankton, SD

Supplies: Cardstock (Bazzill); patterned paper (Fancy Pants); chipboard, rub-ons (BasicGrey); ink (Clearsnap); pen (Uniball); circle punch, decorative edge punch (Fiskars); Misc: ribbon

Inspired Idea!

When designing a two-page layout, pretend there's no break between the two background sheets. The design instantly becomes more cohesive and unified, making the photo placement easier to visualize.

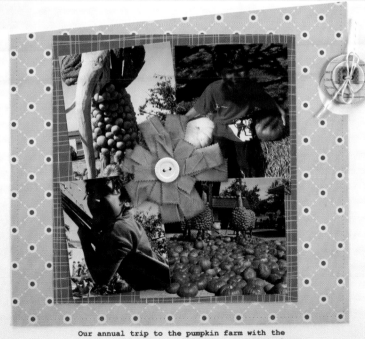

Our annual trip to the pumpkin farm with the Pomsars. The pumpkin elephant was definitely a highlight and after we chose our pumpkins it was a race for the hammock! Jucker Farm Oct 2008

Tradition

Tradition

Hera Frei
Kusnacht, Switzerland

Supplies: Cardstock (Bazzill) patterned paper (Cosmo Cricket); lettering (Pink Paislee, BasicGrey); fabric flower (Pink Paislee); chipboard buttons (Jenni Bowlin); pearls (Kaisercraft); circle punch (Creative Memories); Misc: baker's twine, Artisan font

Nolan at the Patch

Rebecca Wilken
Granbury, TX

Supplies: Software (Corel); papers by Michelle Coleman (Little Dreamer Designs); template [modified] by Janet Phillips (The Daily Digi); large photo overlay by Lynn Favreau (CatScrap); circle frame by Katie Pertiet (Designer Digitals); doodles by Kate Hadfield (Lilypad); acrylic letters by Emily Powers (Oscraps); Misc: SP Holy Guacamole font

Inspired Idea!

If you're toying with the idea of trying digital, why not start with a template? Digital templates are incredibly versatile and easy to use, and once you get the hang of it, you can alter them to make them uniquely yours like Rebecca has done here. Replacing the squares with circles on the right half of the page gives the layout its own unique flair.

Carving the Pumpkin

Tracey Taylor
Grand Bay-Westfield, NB

Supplies: Cardstock (Bazzill); patterned paper (My Little Shoebox, Creative Imaginations, Jillibean Soup); die-cut paper (Creative Imaginations); transparency (Making Memories); chipboard pumpkin (Riff Raff); letters (Jenni Bowlin, Scenic Route); ribbon, trinket pin (Making Memories), stamps (myStamp BOX), brads (Queen & Co); Misc: buttons

Picking Pumpkins
Wendi Manuel-Scott
Leesburg, VA

Supplies: Cardstock (Bazzill, Studio Calico, Kraft); patterned paper (My Mind's Eye, October Afternoon, Sassafras Lass); letters (American Crafts); flowers (Sassafras Lass); labels (Studio Calico, Jenny Bowlin); stitched brads (BasicGrey); calendar tags (Elle Studio)

Carve It!
Sarah de Guzman
Sunnyvale, CA

Supplies: Cardstock (Bazzill); patterned paper (Teresa Collins); letters (American Crafts); gems (Want2Scrap); fun tape (Kiki Art); punch (Marvy Uchida); Misc: pen

Spooky
Stephanie Wheeler
Chattanooga, TN

Supplies: Cardstock (Pink Paislee); patterned paper (Daisy D's, The Paper Company); letters (Making Memories); stickers (Paper Studio, Jenni Bowlin); crepe paper (Jenni Bowlin); pen (FaberCastell), ink (StazOn); punch (Fiskars); Misc: glitter mist, thread

The Costume

Angela J. Prieto
Stockton, KS

Supplies: Patterned papers, rub-ons, letters (BoBunny); journaling die-cut (Jillibean Soup); labels (Dymo)

2 white sheets torn in strips

1 pair of white gloves

1 pair of white socks

Countless hours of hand stitching

Pricking my fingers over & over

So worth it all to see the look on your face when I finally finished your mummy costume. Oct. 2008

I d' Cap'ain

Carol Monson
Las Vegas, NV

Supplies: Patterned paper (Pink Paislee, Creative Imaginations, Cosmo Cricket); labels (Making Memories); letters (Pink Paislee, Making Memories, American Crafts); rub-ons, brad (Pink Paislee); Misc: thread, ink, pen

Prrrfect

Jennifer Wuthrich
Evans, CO

Supplies: Cardstock (Bazzill); patterned paper, die cut (Pink Paislee); stickers (American Craft); Misc: Arial font

Inspired Idea!

A great way to create a focal point photo is by adding a strip of smaller, supporting photos to the layout. This photo strip, showcasing additional shots from the same day, highlights the larger photo without being distracting. What a wonderful way to add some of your favorite outtakes from a photo shoot!

Costume Dragon

Jing-Jing Nickel
Roseville, MN

Supplies: Cardstock (Bazzill); patterned paper, stickers (Reminisce); rub-on (Making Memories); scallop and border cutter (Purple Cows); pen (American Crafts)

Thanksgiving

Gretchen McElveen
(Memory Makers Master, 2009)
Helena, AL

Supplies: Patterned paper (BasicGrey, Making Memories, My Mind's Eye); brads (American Crafts, Making Memories); chipboard (KI Memories, Making Memories); die-cuts (QuicKutz); journaling block (Jenni Bowlin); stickers (7gypsies, Making Memories); Misc: corner rounder, pen

So Much to be Thankful For

Jennifer Wuthrich
Evans, CO

Supplies: Software (Adobe Photoshop CS3); papers, elements (Shabby Princess); template by Crystal Wilkerson (Jessica Sprague); Misc: Arial font, Digs My Hart font

We all went to Mom's & George's first and had brunch. Then we went to Juli and Greg's new house and Missy, Juli, and I made a delicious Thanksgiving feast. Brian and Joey were very helpful and fun and I loved being in the kitchen with my sisters. We laughed at You Tube videos while we cooked. A good time was had by all!

Nov. 26, 2009

Inspired Idea!

We've all got those not-so-great photos. Cute expressions with way too much going on in the background. Don't trash those pictures—crop them! Cut away the excess and you're left with priceless shots that, when assembled together, create the perfect collage of memories from your family event.

Thankful

Kathleen Summers
Roseville, CA

Supplies: Cardstock, papers, overlays by Katie Pertiet (Designer Digitals); worn page edges by Lynn Grieveson (Designer Digitals); stitched scallop border, white stitching, LoopDaLoop brush, Blessing WordArt by Anna Aspnes (Designer Digitals); photo clusters, photo wrap, journaler, brown stitching, paper leaves by Katie Pertiet (Designer Digitals); words (Ali Edwards)

Being Thankful

Beth Gerlach
Milwaukee, WI

Supplies: Cardstock (Bazzill); patterned paper, letters, die-cut stickers (Bella Blvd); Misc: ink, buttons, thread

Spotlight On...

Kimber McGray
Carmel, IN

Kimber McGray

is the author of *Scrapbook Secrets* and *175 Fresh Card Ideas*. Inside *Scrapbook Secrets*, get the scoop on 50 simple secrets that will help you scrap better, scrap faster and have fun along the way. *175 Fresh Card Ideas* is packed with card designs and step-by-step instructions for all occasions so you'll never be stuck without an idea for any card-giving occasion.

Sweet Summer

Supplies: Cardstock (Core'dinations); patterned paper, stickers (Cosmo Cricket); journaling spot (Jillibean Soup); letters (American Crafts); foam adhesive (3L Scrapbook Adhesives); pen (Martha Stewart Crafts)

Homemade Treats

Supplies: Cardstock (Core'dinations, Jillibean Soup); patterned paper (BasicGrey, October Afternoon); letters (American Crafts); stickers (October Afternoon); punch (We R Memory Keepers, Stampin' UP!); foam adhesive (3L Scrapbook Adhesives); floss (DMC); pen (Martha Stewart Crafts)

Fun!

Annika Bergquist
Oskarshamn, Sweden

*Supplies: Cardstock (Bazzill); patterned paper
(S.E.I.); chipboard (Sense); stickers (American
Craft); brad (Panduro); Misc: pen, punch,
pearlmaker, punchinella, scissors*

Barbeque in the Snow

Anna Björklund
Strangnas, Sweden

*Supplies: Cardstock (Bazzill); patterned paper (BoBunny,
Pink Paislee); flowers, flower centers, lace (Prima);
letters (Adornit); overlay (Hamby); pearls (Kaisercraft);
Misc: sewing machine, ink, Cocoa Daisy kit*

I Love Snow

Trisha Hill
Breckenridge, TX

*Supplies: Cardstock (Bazzill); patterned paper
(Black Market Paper Society, Piggy Tales); felt strip
(Queen & Co); chipboard snowflakes (Creative
Imaginations); letters (American Crafts); snowflake
brads (Spare Parts); ink (StazOn)*

Inspired Idea!

Just because you're using a decorative edged sheet of cardstock for your background doesn't mean you can't line your photos up with the edge. Simply position them where you want them, flip the page over and cut the scallop (or other shape) right into your photos. The result is a clever design element that will add fun to your new layout!

Snow Pals

Donna Brisbois
Princeton, MA

Supplies: Patterned paper (BoBunny, Daisy D's) die-cuts (BoBunny); chipboard title (American Crafts); crochet flowers (Bazzill); brads (BasicGrey); gemstones (Martha Stewart Crafts); date sticker (October Afternoon); border punch (Fiskars); Misc: journaling pen, metallic marker

My Snow Angel

Dee Gallimore-Perry
Griswold, CT

Supplies: Cardstock, patterned papers, cut outs, stickers, jewels, rub-on (BoBunny); Misc: foam squares, Century Gothic font

Snowman Time

Iara Gomes-Baer
Gummersbach, Germany

Supplies: Paper, snowman, frames, brads, flowers, tags: Snowman Happy by Kate Teague (Two Peas in a Bucket); journaling space brushes v.2 by Sande Krieger (Two Peas in a Bucket); snowflakes by Baers Garten Designs (Scrapbook Graphics); string by Designs by Lily (The Lilypad); essential stitches 1 by Syrin (CatScrap)

Let It Snow

Liana Suwandi
Wylie, TX

Supplies: Cardstock (Bazzill); patterned paper, buttons, paper clips, clear transparency, sticker (Fancy Pants); border punch (Fiskars); jewel (EK success); hand-cut snowmen (from patterned paper by Fancy Pants); rub-ons (Fancy Pants); paper cutter (Purple Cows); adhesive (Xyron); Misc: GF Halda Normal font

The Sweet Taste of Snow

Kelly Waterman
Louisville, KY

Supplies: Cardstock, liquid glass (Close to My Heart, Bazzill); patterned paper (BoBunny); letters (Pressed Petals); buttons (ChatterBox, Close to My Heart); rub-ons (Making Memories); crystals (Queen and Co); Misc: pen, embossing powder, thread

Inspired Idea!

If you'd love to start playing with your pictures but don't have money in the budget for an expensive photo editing program, try your hand at some of the free online programs like Picnik. You can upload your photos and try out a variety of different effects on them with no risk to your pictures…or your wallet!

Hidden Meat Balls?

Nicole Martel
Crownsville, MD

Supplies: Patterned paper (October Afternoon, Pink Paislee, Graphic 45); Kraft paper (Bazzill); snowflakes, buttons, tag (Making Memories); thickers (American Crafts); ribbon (Maya Road); punch (Martha Stewart Crafts); adhesive (Beacon Adhesives); Misc: black pen

Festival of Lights 2009

Wendy Zullo
Middlebury, CT

Supplies: Paper, beads, word tags by Aja Abney and Gabi (Scrap Artist); title, menorah by Kate Hadfield (The Lilypad); photo frames, staples by Katie Pertiet (Designer Digitals); paper tear by Anna Aspnes (Designer Digitals); Misc: American Typewriter font

Chatting with Santa

Nicole Stark
(Memory Makers Master, 2007)
Roy, UT

Supplies: Cardstock (Bazzill); patterned paper (Making Memories, Crate Paper); embossing folder (Provo Craft); stamps (Studio Calico); date card (Jenni Bowlin); letters, definitions, paper leaves, glitter (Making Memories); chipboard tree (BasicGrey); pearls (Kaisercraft); ink (Ranger); Misc: vintage ledger paper

Letter to Santa

Dee Gallimore-Perry
Griswold, CT

Supplies: Patterned paper (BoBunny); cardstock stickers (KI Memories, Scenic Route, October Afternoon, Heidi Grace, BoBunny); gem (KI Memories); brads (BoBunny); rub-on (Chatterbox); die-cut journaling block (Fancy Pants); Misc: Century Gothic font

Sleepy Head Santa Girl

Becky Williams
Wolfforth, TX

Supplies: Patterned paper, chipboard, journal spots, die-cuts (Collage Press); stickers (Cosmo Cricket, American Crafts); pearls (Prima)

Feast of the 7 Fishes

Amy Tan
Culver City, CA

Supplies: Patterned paper (Studio Calico); letters, stickers (Studio Calico, American Crafts); rub-ons (American Crafts); Misc: pen

Traditions

Donna Jannuzzi
San Diego, CA

Supplies: Cardstock (Bazzill); patterned paper (Making Memories, October Afternoon, Creative Imaginations); letters (BasicGrey); stickers, buttons, felt accent, brad (Making Memories); metal accents (Bazzill, Blue Moon Beads); tag (Paper Source); tickets (Creative Cafe); paper clip (Tim Holtz); chipboard star (Kelly Panacci); Misc: star punch, flower punch, twine

Presents

Rochelle Spears
Anaheim, CA

Supplies: Cardstock (Bazzill); patterned paper (My Mind's Eye); flowers (Prima); letters (American Crafts); tape (Dymo); Misc: chipboard tag, ribbon, brads, ink, staples, glitter mist

Celebrate the Season

Cindy Childress
Westminster, MD

Supplies: Cardstock (DCWV); patterned paper (BasicGrey, DCWV); letters, numbers (K&Co); brads (Making Memories); shapes (Ranger); Misc: scissors, buttons, thread, flower, ink

Story Hour Party

Amy Wheeler
Cecilia, KY

Supplies: Cardstock (Bazzill); patterned paper (Crate Paper, American Crafts); chipboard (Bazzill, Crate Paper); letters (American Crafts, Chatterbox); stickers (Crate Paper); rick rack (May Arts); Misc: pen, edge distresser

Comfort and Joy

Melissa Ferguson
Victoria, British Columbia

Supplies: Cardstock (C'ordinations, Bazzill); patterned paper (Bella Blvd); chipboard stars (BasicGrey); letters (American Crafts); brads (Karen Foster, BasicGrey); stickers (Bella Blvd); Misc: ink, adhesive foam, bling

Country Outing

Victoria Murray
Toronto, Ontario

Supplies: Software (Adobe); patterned paper, letters, buttons (BasicGrey); labels by Andrea Victoria (Designer Digitals); edge distresser (Tonic); Misc: ink, embroidery floss

Year 2010

Loredana Bucaria
Quarto Napoli, Italy

Supplies: Cardstock (Bazzill); patterned paper (Scenic Route, October Afternoon, 7gypsies); chipboard frames (Making Memories); letters, numbers (American Crafts, Scenic Route, Making Memories, BoBunny); stamps (American Crafts, Florileges); scissors (Fiskars); embellishments (American Crafts, Tattered Angels, Heidi Swapp); Misc: glitter mist, scallop square, heart punches, stapler, brown ink pad, slick pen, buttons, fabric, ticket, pin, package paper, white cotton thread, glue

Inspired Idea!

Who says a layout has to have a photo? For a layout about the upcoming year, creating a photo-less page is perfectly acceptable. Instead of focusing on the photo, focus on the meaning behind the page—the journaling and a few little details are all you need to create a memorable scrapbooking page.

New Year's Countdown

Ashley C. Riley
New Orleans, LA

Supplies: Patterned paper (Scenic Route); letters (Scenic Route, American Crafts); label maker (Dymo)

Year 2009

Serena Gedlaman
Calgary, Alberta

Supplies: Cardstock (Bazzill); patterned paper, die-cuts (Dream Street Papers); letters (American Craft); chipboard (Scenic Route)

Chinese New Year

Lisa VanderVeen
(Memory Makers Master, 2006)
Santa Monica, CA

Supplies: Software (Adobe Photoshop Elements 7); patterned paper, charm, coin, letters, frame, flowers from Chinese New Year Kit by Allie Llacer (Sweet Shoppe Designs); hemp tie by Katie Pertiet (Designer Digitals)

We arranged to meet up with a bunch of friends from school for the Chinese New Year parade in Chinatown. I have ALWAYS wanted to see the dragons. They exceeded my every expectation. A great day!

XOXO

Ann-Marie Morris
Simi Valley, CA

Supplies: Cardstock (Bazzill); patterned paper (My Mind's Eye, American Crafts, October Afternoon); letters (Cosmo Cricket); bingo card (Jenni Bowlin); rub-ons (Hambly); stamps (Hampton Art, Autumn Leaves); ribbon (Wyla); Misc: pen, buttons, punches, staples, ink, pin

Magical

Glenda Tkalac
Moose Jaw, Saskatchewan

Supplies: Patterned paper (My Minds Eye); acetate embellies (K&Co); chipboard (KI Memories, Scenic Route); glitter mist (Tattered Angels); acrylic heart (Making Memories); gel pen (MultiCraft Imports); ink (Tsukineko); Misc: metal word

Inspired Idea!

Use squares of patterned paper to create a homey, paper quilt on your next layout. The lined-up squares, mixed in with the same sized photos will give your layout a comfy feel right off the bat! Add a few hand stitches and you've got a quilted page of perfection. Experiment with different sizes and patterns for a variety of looks you're sure to love!

Love

Gretchen McElveen
(Memory Makers Master, 2009)
Helena, AL

Supplies: Patterned paper (BasicGrey, My Little Shoebox, My Mind's Eye); brads (American Crafts); letters (Heidi Swapp/ Advantus); chipboard hearts (Making Memories); Misc: pen, ink, acrylic paint, embroidery floss

Inspired Idea!

A plastic template is a great little tool—and so versatile! Using it as a stencil and spraying it with colored mist is a fun way to add dimension to your layout like Laura's done here. Create your own backgrounds by experimenting with templates and other mediums, like ink, paint and even glitter and glue.

My Funny Valentine

Laura Achilles
Littleton, CO

Supplies: Cardstock (Bazzill); patterned paper (Dream Street Papers); rub-ons (Dream Street Papers, Doodlebug); letters (American Crafts, Making Memories); template (Crafters Workshop); rubber stamp (Purple Onion); fiber (Martha Stewart Crafts); glitter mist (Tattered Angels); Misc: adhesive, ink, punch, vintage dictionary page

Crafting Valentines

Paula Gilarde
Bedford, MA

Supplies: Cardstock (Core'dinations); letters (BoBunny); ticket, chipboard button (Jenni Bowlin); pin (Fancy Pants, Maya Road); software (Adobe Photoshop CS2); frame by Katie Pertiet (Designer Digitals)

Spotlight On...

Sherry Steveson
Wilmington, NC

Sherry Steveson
is the author of *When Life Gives You Lemons* and *The Scrapbook Embellishment Handbook*. *When Life Gives You Lemons* gives you tips and techniques for hiding and making the most of photo flaws. Plus, get tips for fixing photos using Photoshop Elements. *The Scrapbook Embellishment Handbook* is your go-to guide for dressing up your layouts with 51 illustrated techniques and more than 120 ideas for using 17 types of embellishments.

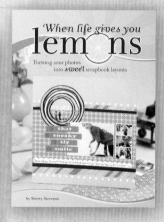

Spring Ahead

Supplies: Cardstock (Bazzill); patterned paper (Fancy Pants, Collage Press, Crate Paper); chipboard (BoBunny); mist (Tattered Angels); letters (American Crafts); Misc: mesh, brads

Perfect Day

Supplies: Cardstock, patterned paper (Core'dinations, Autumn Leaves); letters (Making Memories); die-cut (KI Memories); Misc: glitter, jewels

Believe

Chrissy Joester
Queensland, Australia

Supplies: Cardstock (Bazzill); letters (American Crafts); flowers (Green Tara); butterfly (Spotlight); pearl buckle (Bella!); ribbon (Birch); gems (Kaisercraft); chipboard (My Mind's Eye); heart gem (BasicGrey); pink scalloped sticker (October Afternoon); Misc: acrylic paint, glitter mist, oval mirror, metal frames, C charm

Baptism

Kathleen Summers
Roseville, CA

Supplies: Classic cardstock, watery wings brush, buttons, letters by Katie Pertiet, papers by Lynn Grieveson, acrylic elements by Pattie Knox, stitching by Anna Aspnes (Designer Digitals); handdrawn words by Ali Edwards;

Congrats

Jennifer McCracken
Loveland, OH

Supplies: Cardstock (Bazzill); patterned paper (MAMBI); brads (Making Memories); die-cuts (MAMBI); ribbons (Doodlebug, KI Memories); Misc: pen

Inspired Idea!

The rule of threes will never let you down! As you're designing, keep in mind that adding in three of the same element in a visual triangle will instantly please the eye. Take the photos and the circles on this layout—they each form their own visual triangle, creating a well-designed page that leads your eye just where it needs to go. This is an easy, tried and true rule that won't let you down!

I Did It

Sarah de Guzman
Sunnyvale, CA

Supplies: Cardstock (Bazzill); patterned paper (Imaginisce); letters (American Crafts); stickers (Jenni Bowlin); journal tags (Jillibean Soup); decorative tape (Prima); Misc: pen

{Happy Birthday!}

Celebrating He's Three

Deana Boston
O'Fallon, MO

Supplies: Cardstock (Recollections); patterned paper, chipboard stickers, letters (Cosmo Cricket); stickers (SRM Press, Cosmo Cricket); Misc: baker's twine, pen, Century Gothic font

The Birthday Splash

Christa Paustenbaugh
Camp Lejeune, NC

Supplies: Cardstock (Bazzill); patterned paper (American Crafts, Studio Calico, October Afternoon, Sassafras Lass); chipboard circle (Maya Road); letters (American Crafts); corrugated letters/numbers (Jillibean Soup); sticker (MAMBI); paper flower (Prima); brads (My Mind's Eye); buttons (Sassafras Lass); rub-ons (K&Co); Misc: pen

Make a Wish

Donna Jannuzzi
San Diego, CA

Supplies: Cardstock (Bazzill); patterned paper (Martha Stewart Crafts); letters (Heidi Swapp); Misc: acrylic paint, star punch, photo corner punch

Inspired Idea!

Take some time to have a little fun with your patterned paper. Try sculpting it in different shapes like Emeline did here. Her handmade circular embellishment at the center of her layout is made out of small scraps of paper rolled into small cones. It's a playful addition to her layout, but best of all, it's completely one of a kind.

Celebrate

Emeline Seet
Singapore

Supplies: Cardstock (Bazzill); patterned paper (The Girls Paperie); stickers (K&Co, October Afternoon); pearls (Melissa Frances); Misc: ribbon

Birthday Bass

Beth Hallgren
Hartford, MI

Supplies: Cardstock (DCWV, Bazzill); patterned paper (My Mind's Eye, BasicGrey); letters (BasicGrey, American Crafts, Making Memories); rub-ons (BasicGrey); brads (Paper Studio, Making Memories); punch (McGill); pen (Sakura); adhesive (Tombow); Misc: floss, fish hook, Georgia font

Birthday Boy

Jenn Koss
Kingman, KS

Supplies: Cardstock (Paper Studio, DCWV), paper, stickers (Sassafras Lass), letters (Jenni Bowlin, American Crafts); die-cut (Spellbinders), embossing elements (Provo Craft); Misc: pen, distress ink, scissors, adhesive

Happy First

Melissa Rhodes
Idaho Falls, ID

Supplies: Software (Adobe Photoshop Elements 6); paper (Design By Dani); WordArt (Lauren Grier); element by Erica Hernandez (Two Peas in a Bucket); journal block (unknown)

A Happy Birthday

Rebecca Wilken
Granbury, TX

Supplies: Software (Corel); paper by Dianne Rigdon (Scrapbook Graphics); template [modified], mask by Anna Aspnes (Designer Digitals); birthday stamp, journal stamp by Katie Pertiet (Designer Digitals); Misc: Pea Steve font

Inspired Idea!

Handwritten journaling is a wonderful, personal touch to add to any scrapbook layout, and adding guidelines to ensure you don't write at an angle doesn't have to be boring. Consider running your layout through your sewing machine without any thread in the needle to create lines with a decorative element.

Cupcakes and Coffee

Ann-Marie Morris
Simi Valley, CA

Supplies: Cardstock (Bazzill, DCWV); patterned paper (October Afternoon, Cosmo Cricket); letters (Cosmo Cricket, Making Memories, Jenni Bowlin); rub-ons (American Crafts); chipboard (Tim Holtz); rhinestones (Darice); ribbon (Wyla); Misc: buttons, pen, pin, acrylic paint, punches, measuring tape, fabric, staples, thread, vintage paper

Celebrating

Natalie Erin Strand
Champaign, IL

Supplies: Cardstock (Paper Reflections); patterned paper, brads (Making Memories, Paper Studio); acrylic stamps (Making Memories); punches (Fiskars, Martha Stewart Crafts), die-cutting machine (Silhouette); Misc: gel pen, machine stitching, ribbon, stamping ink, Wendy Medium font

The Best Present

Ronda Palazzari
(Memory Makers Master, 2009)
Thornton, CO

Supplies: Cardstock (Bazzill); patterned paper (BasicGrey, Crate Paper); chipboard framers (American Crafts); stamps (Purple Onion); flowers (Maya Road); rub-on (Jenni Bowlin); ephemera (K&Co); letters (American Crafts, Adornit); pin (Tim Holtz); Misc: pen, ink, punch, ribbon/ seam binding

Being 30 Today!

Connie Hyde Mercer
Belmont, TX

Supplies: Patterned paper (BasicGrey); flower (Prima); journal paper (Jenni Bowlin); calendar card (Jillibean Soup); letters (American Crafts, Making Memories); trim (Creative Imaginations); Misc: pen, buttons, baker's twine, memorabilia, border punch

Celebration

Amy Martin
(Memory Makers Master, 2009)
Corpus Christi, TX

Supplies: Software (Corel PaintShopPro vXI); letters by Audrey Neal (Oscraps); bookplate, wordstrips by Emily Powers (Oscraps); brads by Meredith Fenwick (Two Peas In A Bucket); buttons by Amy Hutchinson and Michelle Coleman (After Five Designs, Little Dreamer Designs); frames, overlays (Something Blue Studios, CatScrap); flowers by Camila Designs (After Five Designs); heart by Jacque Larsen (The Lilypad); paper bits by Anne deJong (Funky Playground); paper overlay, acrylic paint by CD Muckosky (Little Dreamer Designs); WordArt by Paislee Press (Oscraps); Misc: MaszynaAEG font

Inspired Idea!

The white space in this photo offers prime embellishment real estate! Instead of building the cluster of decorative items around the entire perimeter of the photo, overlap right on the white space. This kind of layering pulls everything in together and leads the eye to the focal point picture.

A Love Story

Stephanie Wheeler
Chattanooga, TN

Supplies: Cardstock (October Afternoon); patterned paper (Cosmo Cricket, vintage); chipboard (Maya Road); card (Jenni Bowlin); stickers (Jenni Bowlin, BasicGrey); pen (American Crafts); stamps (BasicGrey, vintage); Misc: buttons, pearls, pin, flower

Love Today and Always

Janine Buckles
London, Ontario

*Supplies: Software (Photoshop Elements 5.0);
actions, digital brushes, embellishments, flowers,
frame, papers (Scrap Girls)*

And Two Become One

Renee' Morris-Dezember
Richland, WA

*Supplies: Software (Photoshop 6.0); digital template
(Manda Girl); digital papers, label by CreativityByCrystal
(Jessica Sprague); vintage stacked flowers by Kitschy
Digitals (Jessica Sprague); stitches by Sande Krieger
(Two Peas in a Bucket)*

I Do

Chrys Q. Rose
Tracy, CA

*Supplies: Cardstock (Bazzill); patterned paper
(Crate, October Afternoon, Pink Paislee); brads
(Boxer Scrapbook); die-cut (Collage Press); jour-
nal card (Maya Road); rub-ons (Maya Road,
BasicGrey, Déjà Views)*

Chapter Four:

SPECIAL RELATIONSHIPS

Very often the memories we hold the dearest are enriched by the people we share them with. Our birthdays are more meaningful because of the people who help us celebrate. Our vacations are happier because we shared them with our family. From the sweet relationship we have with our newborn baby to the sometimes volatile relationship we share with an adult sibling, the special people we know make our lives worth living.

This chapter will fill you up with ideas on how to capture the relationships that are most important to you. You may even find yourself wanting to create a page about someone you never thought would appear in one of your scrapbooks. A teacher who inspired you years ago. A relative you never met. Someone who broke your heart but ended up changing you for the better. Your life is a wealth of stories—and those stories usually have key players. Don't forget to include them on your pages—it's the only way to truly tell the whole story.

Snapshots of a Family

Terri Hayes
Cary, NC

Supplies: Cardstock (Bazzill); patterned paper (American Crafts, October Afternoon, My Little Shoebox); trim (Webster's Pages); stickers (American Crafts, BasicGrey, My Little Shoebox, October Afternoon); Misc: pen

Buildin' Block

Sarah de Guzman
Sunnyvale, CA

Supplies: Cardstock (Core'dinations); patterned paper (Jillibean Soup); letters (American Crafts); butterfly embellishments (Jenni Bowlin); Misc: pen, twine, foam adhesive

Inspired Idea!

A little bit of creativity can stretch your supplies a long, long way. For this layout, a number "8" letter sticker easily became the capital "S" in the title with just a few simple snips. With a few small changes, an "F" can become an "L", an "E" can become an "F" and depending on the font, the numbers can become all kinds of letters! Don't assume you don't have what you need until you've exhausted every possibility!

I Spy

Michelle Houghton
Clive, IA

Supplies: Cardstock (Archiver's); patterned paper (BasicGrey, Deja Views); letters (American Crafts); chipboard bird (BasicGrey); tag (Wall Mart); Misc: pen, floss

A Year Can Make

Meg Barker
Detroit Lakes, MN

Supplies: Patterned paper (Crate Paper, My Minds Eye); letters (Hambly); stickers (Heidi Grace); Misc: pen, fabric

Just Us

Katherine Blue
Elkridge, MD

Supplies: Cardstock (Bazzill); patterned paper (My Mind's Eye); letters (Jenni Bowlin); trim (GCD Studios); brad (Imaginisce); chipboard numbers (American Crafts); pearls (Prima); pen (Signo); punch (Fiskars); quote (Cloud Nine); ribbon (Offray); Misc: thread, pin

Inspired Idea!

When you have several faces to fit on one page, do a little creative cropping. Don't worry about chopping off an ear (or two), the face is the most important part. By getting in close, you're able to arrange so many more photos than you would otherwise. Plus, the eye is instantly drawn to the beautiful faces you're showing off!

So Blessed

Julie Gordon
Carramar, Western Australia

Supplies: Cardstock (Bazzill); patterned paper (Kaisercraft, My Mind's Eye); letters (American Crafts, BasicGrey); stickers (Making Memories); flowers (Chelley Bean Designs); leaves (Prima); pearls (Kaisercraft, Prima); trinket pin (Maya Road); Misc: ribbon

Finally 4

Jill Cornell
Windsor Heights, IA

Supplies: Cardstock (Bazzill); patterned paper (October Afternoon, Bella Blvd., Making Memories); letters (Pink Paislee); chipboard hearts (Heidi Swapp); chipboard people (Maya Road); rhinestones (Melissa Frances); sticker (October Afternoon, American Crafts); Misc: thread, ink, punch, decorative scissors

We prayed for years to add to our family and were surprised (but blessed) to become an instant family of 4.

finally 4

it doesn't get any better than this

Hooray for My Family

Glenda Tkalac
Moose Jaw, SK

Supplies: Patterned paper (We R Memory Keepers, Scenic Route, DCWV); die-cuts (Cosmo Cricket); journal stickers (Colorbök); chipboard cheerleader (Magistical Memories); chipboard circle (Scenic Route); flower (Heidi Swapp); rick rack (Offray); die-cut letters (Making Memories); Misc: notepaper, acrylic paint

happy

Hello Sunshine!

Hooray for my family!!

love

Sweet Baby

Christyn Holmes
Littleton, CO

Supplies: Cardstock (Bazzil); patterned paper (Sassafras Lass, Studio Calico); wood ceneer die-cut (Studio Calico); stickers (Sassafras Lass); Software (Adobe); Word Art by Ali Edwards (Designer Digitals); Misc: buttons, baker's twine, glimmer mist, ink

Awesome Mommy

Teresa G. Fenstermacher
Telford, PA

Supplies: Cardstock (DCWV); patterned paper (BasicGrey); distress ink (Tim Holtz); glitter mist (Tattered Angels); paper ribbon (K&Co); die-cuts, rub-ons (BasicGrey); butterfly punch (Martha Stewart Crafts); brads (Imaginisce); pearls (Recollections); Misc: adhesive, pen

Wonder

Sandi Minchuk
Merrillville, IN

Supplies: Cardstock (Bazzill); patterned paper (Crate Paper, SEI); chipboard tag, photo mat (K&Co); die-cuts (SEI); letters (Doodlebug, Making Memories); Misc: pens, edge distresser, glass beads, machine stitching, thread, adhesive

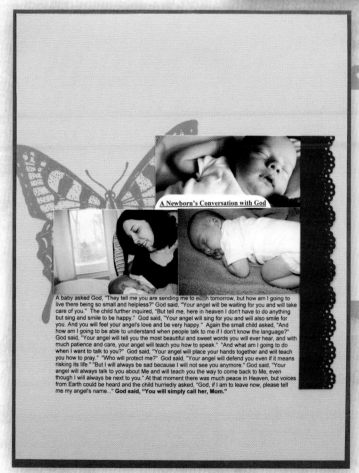

Inspired Idea!

Sometimes the journaling drives your layout. When you've got a great story to tell, consider printing the text first and then build your layout around it. Once the words are in place, you can determine photo size, placement and what embellishments will help best convey the emotion and the story you're looking to capture.

A Newborn's Conversation with God

Nicole Martel
Crownsville, MD

Supplies: Cardstock (Couture Cardstock); rub-on (Jenni Bowlin)

Love Your Laughter

Anna Koziarek
Zielonka, Mazowiekie, Poland

Supplies: Patterned paper, chipboard, flowers, leaves, stickers, bling, studs, pearls, pebbles, transparency (Prima); Distress Stickles (Ranger); Misc: Prima packaging, fine scissors, adhesive foam

Share

Wendy Kwok
Singapore

Supplies: Cardstock (Bazzill Basics); patterned paper (Graphic 45); flowers, leaves (Prima); chipboard frame, pins (Maya Road); word stickers (7gypsies); letters (American Crafts); trims (Making Memories and Prima Marketing)

Inspired Idea!

Looking to try out a handwritten title, but lack the confidence? Build up the courage by first creating your handwritten element on a separate sheet of paper or cardstock and then cut it out. If you mess it up, there's no harm done—simply take out a new sheet and start over! Pretty soon, you'll be coming up with all kinds of fun new titles that are completely original.

Being Your Mom

Bethany Kartchner
Laveen, AZ

Supplies: Cardstock (Bazzill); patterned paper (Harmonie); chipboard award, frame (Sassafras Lass); chipboard bird (American Crafts); stamps (Hero Arts, Stampotique, Heidi Swapp); letters, overlay clouds (My Little Shoebox); flower (Prima); acrylic paint (Shimmerz Blingz); Misc: ink, pen, transparency, scissors, bling

Love You Mom

Carly Blaiss
Alpharetta, GA

Supplies: Patterned paper (Graphic 45, GCD Studios, Making Memories, K&Co); tag (GCD Studios); stickers (K&Co, Jenni Bowlin, Sassafras Lass, 7gypsies); chipboard (K&Co, Making Memories); transparency (Making Memories)

Love the look of a linear layout, but itching to try something new? Marry the linear with a distressed look for a completely new style. Kathleen's layout combines a rectangular set of elements within a square within a square. The placement is clean, but she adds grungy embellishments and distressed edges for an unexpected pop.

Change

Kathleen Summers
Roseville, CA

Supplies: Cardstock, letters, hinge, pinned notes, photo wrap by Katie Pertiet (Designer Digitals); papers by Lynn Grieveson, Mindy Terasawa and Katie Pertiet (Designer Digitals); page edges, buttons by Lynn Grieveson; stitching by Anna Aspnes (Designer Digitals); digital brushes by Katie Pertiet and Anna Aspnes (Designer Digitals)

As Good As It Gets

Wendy Hackney Baisden
Williamson, WV

Supplies: Cardstock (Bazzill); patterned paper (unkown); letters (Provo Craft); flowers (Pettaloo); flies, dragonflies (template by Wendy Hackney Baisden); glitter (Ranger); tag (Dymo); jewels (Studio 18); Misc; pens

Mother Above All Else

Tatum Woodroffe
Roxby Dawns, South Australia

Supplies: Patterned Paper (Jillibean Soup, Sassafras Lass); letters (Jillibean Soup); rub-ons (Pink Paislee); stamps (Hero Arts); border punch (Fiskars); ribbon (Making Memories), doilies (Sweet Vintage 78); tickets (My Little Shoebox); Misc: luggage tag, thread, ink, butterfly sequin

Inspired Idea!

Adding texture to your layout doesn't have to make it busy! Embellishments that jump off the page but are the same color as the background are a fantastic way to incorporate dimension without overwhelming your photos or other design elements. Instead, they provide the perfect canvas to make the important aspects of your page really shine!

Dear Mummy

Piradee Talvanna
Singapore

Supplies: Cardstock (Bazzill, American Crafts); patterned paper, letters (Jenni Bowlin); ribbon (Maya Road); flower (Prima); pen (American Crafts); Misc: punch, twine, string

Happiness is Made to be Shared

Terri Hayes
Cary, NC

Supplies: Cardstock (Bazzill); patterned paper (Sassafras Lass); rub-ons (Lily Bee, Kaisercraft, K&Co); felt (Prima); rhinestones (Mark Richards); Misc: pen, chipboard

Scared?

Ann Schneider
Rochester, NY

Supplies: Cardstock (The Paper Company); patterned paper (K&Co); letters (American Crafts); rub-ons (DCWV, Heidi Grace); stickers (Creative Cafe, Cosmo Cricket, K&Co, Colorbök); Misc: pen, fabric, feather, thread, gems

Sitting on Dad's Lap

Lynn Warner
Coal Valley, IL

Supplies: Patterned paper (The Girls' Paperie); letters (American Crafts, BasicGrey); pin (Tim Holtz); stamps (Unity Stamp Company, Catslife Press); Misc: grungeboard, glitter mist, pen, ink, flower punch

So many scrapbooking embellishments capture the look of hand-drawn doodles. But why use someone else's doodles when you can use your own? Play around with page frames, photo frames and even funky flowers and swirls and you might stumble upon something worth keeping! The best part is no one else will have it because your doodles are completely one of a kind.

Daddy's Girl

Ingeborg Dijkstra-Verbeek
Berg en Terblijt, Netherlands

Supplies: Cardstock (Bazzill); patterned paper (BasicGrey); stamps (BasicGrey, Kaisercraft); chipboard (A2Z); felt butterfly (Chelley Bean Designs); pearls (Kaisercraft); Misc: acrylic paint, pen, foam squares, watercolor pencils

Steal My Kisses

Katie Burnett
Birmingham, AL

Supplies: Cardstock (unknown); letters (American Crafts, Adornit, October Afternoon); brads (BasicGrey); die-cut mask (Silhouette); felt flowers, sequins (Making Memories); glitter mist (Tattered Angels); pens (American Crafts, Sharpie)

Daddy's Girl

Mary Agatha Aviso
Amadeo, Cavite, Philippines

Supplies: Software (Adobe Photoshop CS3); Sweet Caroline Digital Page Kit by Kristin Cronin-Barrow (Sweet Shoppe Designs); WordArt by Manda Bean (Sweet Shoppe Designs); date bits by Misty Cato (Sweet Shoppe Designs); digital template by Cindy Schneider (Sweet Shoppe Designs)

Alike But Different

Pia Salem-Lopez
Dasmariñas City, Cavite, Philippines

Supplies: Cardstock (American Crafts); patterned paper (Scenic Route, Cosmo Cricket, Kaisercraft); chipboard (Scenic Route, Imagination Project); letters (American Crafts); die-cut sticker (BasicGrey); Misc: pen

He is My Dad

Laina Lamb
Bay Village, OH

Supplies: Cardstock (Archiver's, Bazzill); patterned paper (Scenic Route, Making Memories, October Afternoon); stickers (7gypsies); chipboard (Scenic Route, Heidi Swapp, Li'l Davis); letters (American Crafts, Jenni Bowlin)

Daddy's Toys

Michelle Roudebush
Wabash, IN

Supplies: Cardstock (Bazzill); patterned paper (Chatterbox); digital elements by Fee Jardine (Sweet Shoppe Designs); snaps, signs (Making Memories); Misc: pen, transparency, ArmyChalk font, 2PeasCrate font

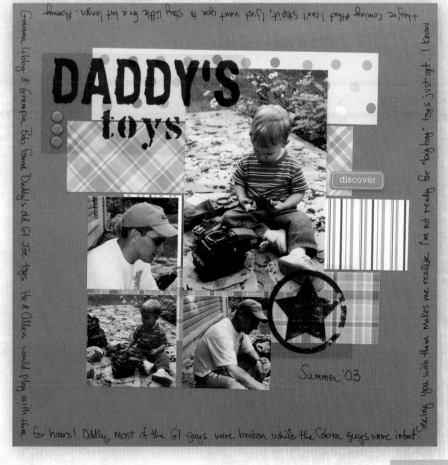

The Good Stuff

Dee Gallimore-Perry
Griswold, CT

Supplies: Patterned paper (BasicGrey, My Mind's Eye, Teresa Collins); chipboard (Teresa Collins, We R Memory Keepers); cardstock stickers (7gypsies); die-cuts (Crate Paper, BoBunny, Cosmo Cricket); flowers (Prima, K&Co); buttons (Lasting Impressions); leaf (BoBunny); Misc: Amanda's Hand font, Type Right! font

Inspired Idea!

Embellishments that seem to float on the page add an interesting depth to your layout. Next time you're looking to make something float, only stitch, staple or glue the top half of the object. The result will be a lovely little shadow underneath the embellishment that will make it stand out from the rest of the page.

Jack & His Daddy

Carol Monson
Las Vegas, NV

Supplies: Patterned paper (Crate Paper, Studio Calico, Making Memories); label (My Mind's Eye); stickers (October Afternoon); ribbon (American Crafts); Misc: brads, button, safety pin, baker's twine, pen, thread

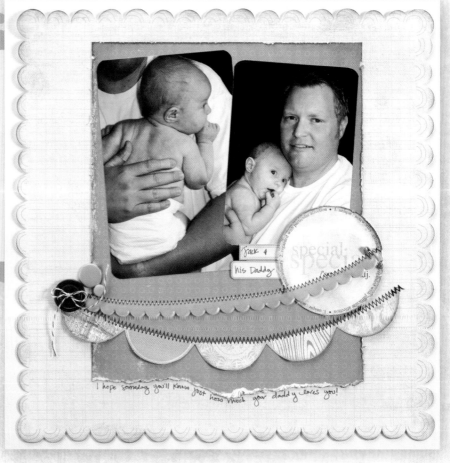

Inspired Idea!

Who says pink is just for girls? Mothers of boys everywhere will be happy to know that pink is perfectly acceptable to use on a boy layout—especially one capturing a tender moment like this one. Steer clear of typical stereotypes and make the pages you want to make, no matter what seems acceptable. Chances are if you love it, everyone else will too!

Sweet

Cindy Childress
Westminster, MD

Supplies: Cardstock, letters (DCWV); patterned paper (K&Co, DCWV, Autumn Leaves); journaling pads (Making Memories); rub-ons (BasicGrey); Misc: pen, punches

Father, Brother, Son

Elisha Barnett
Reading, PA

Supplies: Software (Adobe Photoshop Elements 4.0); patterned paper, WordArt, frame stamp, floral stem by Amanda Sok (Scrap Girls); vellum pocket by Syndee Nuckles (Scrap Girls); envelope by Kerry Schueller (Scrap Girls); metal elements, tab by Amanda Sok (Scrap Girls); frame by Jan Hicks (Scrap Girls); staples by Paula Wright (Scrap Girls); Misc: Traveling Typewriter font, Made font

Brotherhood

Loes de Groot
Appingedamn, Groningen,
Netherlands

Supplies: Patterned paper (Jillibean Soup); felt corner, flower center, butterfly clearstamp (Prima); letters (Rusty Pickle); Misc: ink, thread, buttons, lace, rick rack

Everyday Moments Together

Jamie Harder
Martensville, Saskatchewan

Supplies: Cardstock (Bazzill, Close To My Heart); patterned paper, buttons (Close To My Heart); letters (American Crafts); stamps (Close To My Heart, Glitz Design); glitter mist (Tattered Angels); Misc: waxy floss, paper clip, ink

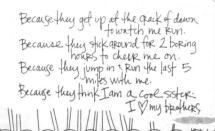

Because they get up at the crack of dawn to watch me run.
Because they stick around for 2 boring hours to cheer me on.
Because they jump in & run the last 5 miles with me.
Because they think I am a cool sister. I ♥ my brothers

they do things like this!

Inspired Idea!

Some elements need a little extra oomph. Next time you're looking to add depth and to make something really stand out, simply outline it with a pen or marker. Letter stickers, journaling blocks and decorative borders all become more interesting to look at when outlined with a thin black marker.

Because

Gretchen McElveen
(Memory Makers Master, 2009)
Helena, AL

Supplies: Patterned paper, chipboard border (My Mind's Eye, Pink Paislee); letters (Pink Paislee); Misc: pen, staples, corner rounder

LIFE IS FOR SHARING

love is for giving

Inspired Idea!

If you're like most scrapbookers, you've probably got a mini album or two lying around with a few incomplete pages inside. If you're not going to get to it, why not use those pages as decorative elements on your next layout? The shape underneath the title on this layout once had a life as a blank mini album page. Now, it's working out nicely as this title's border.

Love is for Sharing

Charity Hassel
Jacksonville, FL

Supplies: Cardstock (Prism); patterned paper, stickers (Little Yellow Bicycle); mini album sheet (October Afternoon); Misc: border punch

For this layout, Staci knew she wanted to spray the background with a water/acrylic paint mix, but she wanted to leave a little white border around the circles. Instead of risking spraying her circular elements, she traced around them and cut out stunt doubles to act as masks for the spot where the real embellishments would later go. Once the page dried, she simply added the circles to the white space and traced around them for a fun, homespun look.

To Her

Staci Etheridge
(Memory Makers Master, 2008)
McKinney, TX

Supplies: Cardstock (The Paper Studio), journaling die-cut (Heidi Swapp), patterned paper (Collage Press, Dream Street Papers), stickers (American Crafts); Misc: acrylic paint, button

Pals

Connie Hyde Mercer
Belmont, TX

Supplies: Patterned paper (Fancy Pants); flowers (Prima); ticket (Jenni Bowlin); trim (Creative Imaginations); letters (American Crafts, Making Memories); Misc: buttons, floss, baker's twine

Noni

Meg Barker
Detroit Lakes, MN

Supplies: Patterned paper (Prima); letters (Li'l Davis); overlays (Hambly); rub-on (Making Memories); stickers (Cosmo Cricket, Heidi Grace); tickets (Tim Holtz); Misc: pen

Never a Dull Moment

Jennifer Evans
Lyons, OR

Supplies: Cardstock (Bazzill); patterned paper (Fancy Pants, We R Memory Keepers, Pink Paislee); chipboard spinner (K&Co); letters (American Crafts); ribbon (Fancy Pants); tag (Making Memories); Misc: corner punch, thread, vintage shirt buttons, watercolor paint, Times New Roman font

Inspired Idea!

Digital scrapbooking is so incredibly versatile. Just one click of the eye-dropper tool in Photoshop and Lisa was able to create a background that perfectly matched the sari her daughter's grandmother is wearing. When matching elements is this easy, there's no reason not to give it a try!

Sophie and her Dadu

Lisa VanderVeen
(Memory Makers Master, 2006)
Santa Monica, CA

Supplies: Cardstock (created by layout artist); patterned paper, flowers, overlays, journaling card, frame by Carina Gardner (Two Peas in a Bucket); button flower, tab, stitching, letters by Crystal Wilkerson (Jessica Sprague); journaling boxes (Two Peas in a Bucket)

September 2009

Sophie and her Dadu

remember when

DAY 03   MONTH 09   YEAR 09

Since moving back to CA, it hasn't been easy to see family as often as we'd like. Sophie hadn't seen Dadu since we moved - almost 2 1/2 years ago. That's too long! We were very happy that we were able to reunite in Skaneateles over Labor Day weekend 2009. It was a wonderful weekend with family and it was long overdue! September 2009.

Skaneateles, NY
Sophie age Six

You Bless My Life.

i ♥ u

Grandma,

You are forever teaching me

about the importance of

FaMiLy

You Bless my Life

Cathy Schellenberg
Steinbach, Manitoba

Supplies: Cardstock (Bazzill); patterned paper, die-cuts, chipboard, (Cosmo Cricket); Misc: sewing machine, Comic Sans font

His Backup

Laina Lamb
Bay Village, OH

Supplies: Cardstock (Bazzill); patterned paper (Scenic Route, KI Memories, K&Co, Making Memories, October Afternoon); pearls (Hero Arts); chipboard (October Afternoon); ribbon (Creative Imaginations, Cosmo Cricket, American Crafts)

Max and my mom Kathy have always been extremely close. I am so happy that even though he is a teenager nothing has changed. Max's friends always ask him, "Why do you hang out with your Grandparents so much?" Max always answers easily, "Because I love them and they are fun to be with." Max knows that whatever he needs, his Grandmother will be there for him. Advice, homework help, vacations away, clothing splurges and more. She helps him so much that I have started to call her his "Backup Mom". Raising three boys is hard work and it is nice to know that when Steve and I are stretched thin as parents, the kids always have their backup parents too. I hope these two always remain this close. November 09

Tia Lucha

Mary Ann Jenkins
Lakewood, CA

Supplies: Cardstock (Bazzill); patterned paper (Cosmo Cricket); letters (American Crafts); date sticker (Jenni Bowlin); Misc: string, punch

You met your Tia Lucha for the first time on Thanksgiving day. You loved sitting in her lap while she sang songs to you in Spanish, and smiled so big when she would call you her bebe bonita.

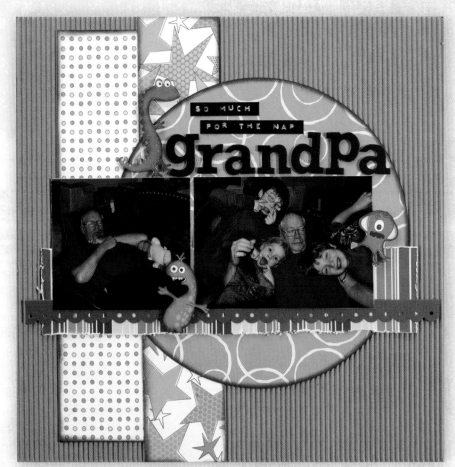

So Much for the Nap Grandpa!

Jill Sarginson
Kanata, Ontario

Supplies: Cardstock (Bazzill); patterned paper (October Afternoon, Scenic Route); corrugated paper (MultiCraft Imports); letters (American Crafts); ink (VersaMark), border punch (Fiskars); label maker, edge distresser (Dymo, Close To My Heart); circle template (Creative Memories)

Inspired Idea!

A great way to add dimension to your next layout is to play around with rubber stamps on your background. By first laying down that layer, you are already promised something interesting to look at underneath all the other elements. This gives you the freedom to add layers stacked on top of each other, each one adding new depth to your page.

With Grandma

Iris Babao Uy
(Memory Makers Master, 2008)
Quezon City, Metro Manila, Philippines

Supplies: Patterned paper, crystal swirls, chipboard, flowers, lace (Prima); metal embellishment (We R Memory Keepers)

Dan and Nan

Debra Fleming
Hamilton, Ontario

Supplies: Cardstock (Bazzill); patterned paper (BasicGrey); letters, numbers, buttons, trims, flowers (Making Memories); leaves (Prima)

You're the Best

Chrys Q. Rose
Tracy, CA

Supplies: Cardstock (Bazzill); patterned paper (October Afternoon); chipboard (Maya Road); brads (Boxer Scrapbook); stamp (Unity); Misc: acrylic paint, ink

Cousins

Armi Custodio
Muntinlupa City, Metro Manila,
Philippines

*Supplies: Software (Adobe);
Noteworthy Collection Biggie by
Syndee Nuckles (Scrap Girls); Collage
Art Collection Biggie by Syndee
Nuckles (Scrap Girls); paper templates
by Dinny Miller (Scrap Girls); brush set
by Brandie Valenzuela (Scrap Girls);
tools, styles by Sarah Batdorf (Scrap
Girls); Misc: Kokila font, Palace Script
MT font, Modern No.20 font, Susie's
Hand font*

Inspired Idea!

Sometimes we're so busy capturing details and expressions we forget to capture the most obviously important photos—like one that showcases three generations (or more.). It's likely these photos will become your most cherished.

3 Gen

Sheredian Vickers
The Woodlands, TX

*Supplies: Cardstock, flower, ribbon
(Bazzill); patterned paper (Scribble
Scrabble, KI Memories); letters (Heidi
Swapp, American Crafts); journaling pad
(Making Memories); bling (DCWV, Paper
Studio); ink (Colorbox); Misc: punches,
adhesive foam, journaling pen, clip*

Childhood Girlfriends

Katharyn Brine
Murrumbateman, Australia

Supplies: Software (Adobe Photoshop Elements 6); cardstock by Anna Aspnes (Designer Digitals); letters, layered template (altered), tree elements by Kitty Designs (Oscraps); flower elements (Kaisercraft); Misc: Myriad Pro font, Clementine Sketch font

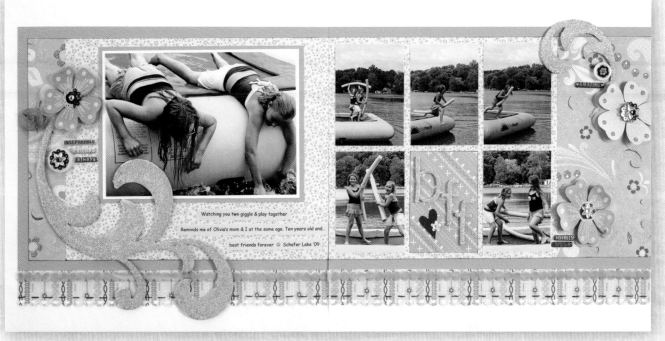

BFF

Beth Hallgren
Hartford, MI

Supplies: Cardstock (Bazzill, DCWV); patterned paper, flowers, acrylic bubble words (K&Co); letters (BasicGrey), flourishes (Fancy Pants); ribbon (Making Memories); glitter (Doodlebug); vellum (American Crafts); punch (EK Success, Fiskars); ink (Clearsnap); adhesive (Tombow, Therm O Web); Misc: floss, Comic Sans MS font

Wish You Here

Loredana Bucaria
Quarto Napoli, Italy

Supplies: Patterned paper (American Crafts); embellishments (American Crafts, 7gypsies, Jenni Bowlin, Elle's Studios); letters, numbers (American Crafts, Making Memories); ribbon (American Crafts, May Arts); Misc: sewing machine, old book paper, scallop scissors, heart scallop punch

Together

Connie Hyde Mercer
Belmont, TX

Supplies: Cardstock (Bazzill); patterned paper, stickers (Jenni Bowlin); letters (American Crafts, Making Memories); chipboard (Scenic Route); trim (Wrights, Creative Imaginations); Misc: pen, staples, buttons, baker's twine, ephemera, border punch

Kisses

Piradee Talvanna
Singapore

Supplies: Cardstock (Bazzill, American Crafts; patterned paper (Graphic 45); stamps (Purple Onion); letters, pen (American Crafts); leaf pin (Maya Road); pearl swirls (Prima); Misc: mist, bling, distress glitter, string

Uncanny

Gretchen McElveen
(Memory Makers Master, 2009)
Helena, AL

Supplies: Cardstock (DMC); patterned paper (KI Memories, My Mind's Eye); bling (Heidi Swapp/Advantus); brads (American Crafts, BasicGrey); die-cuts (My Mind's Eye); flowers (Making Memories); letters (Doodlebug); Misc: staples, pen, ink

Gal Pals

Julie Eickmeier
Tarpon Springs, FL

Supplies: Patterned paper (Prima); letters (American Crafts); buttons (Making Memories); Misc: transparency

Tight

Laura Achilles
Littleton, CO

Supplies: Cardstock (Bazzill); patterned paper, letters (GCD Studios); pearls (Kaisercraft); rub-ons, brads (Doodlebug); fiber (Martha Stewart Crafts); mist (Tattered Angels); Misc: ink, paper doily, punch, pen

Extra! Extra!
SINGLE TO DOUBLE

These layouts show how easy it is to take inspiration from a single-page idea and create a double-page layout.

You Have Each Moment

Patty Hamilton
Mountain View, CA

Supplies: Patterned paper (KI Memories, Webster's Pages); transparency (Hambly); letters (Prima, Little Yellow Bicycle); butterflies (K&Co, Jenni Bowlin); buttons (American Crafts, Jenni Bowlin); die-cut (My Mind's Eye); labels (Jenni Bowlin, Little Yellow Bicycle); stick pin (Maya Road); flashcard (Elle's Studio); chipboard, pebbles, rhinestone bracket (Prima); white appliqué flower (Melissa Frances); flowers (My Mind's Eye, Prima, SEI, K&Co)

Snow Girl

Samantha Walker
(Memory Makers Master, 2005)
Lehi, UT

Supplies: Digital papers and all elements created by Samantha Walker; Misc: Ballpark font, Baskerville font

Oh Boys!

Janis G. Medina-Maghinay
Makati City, Metro Manila, Philippines

Supplies: Cardstock (Bazzill); patterned paper (Fancy Pants); chipboard shapes (Buzz and Bloom); letter (All About Scrapbooking, Buzz and Bloom, Jenni Bowlin), stickers (October Afternoon, 7gypsies), Misc: pen, acrylic paint, chalk, sanding block

Growing Buds

Emeline Seet
Singapore

Supplies: Cardstock (Bazzill); patterned paper (Pebbles); rub-ons (Jenni Bowlin), stickers (American Craft, Jenni Bowlin), Misc: masking tape

Soccer Pals

Suzanna Lee
Glen Allen, VA

Supplies: Cardstock (Bazzill); patterned paper (BoBunny, Prima, Cloud Nine, Colorbök); embellishments (Sassafras Lass, Making Memories, Imagination Project, Li'l Davis, Luxe, Adornit, Scenic Route); trim (Doodlebug, KI Memories); Misc: ink, pen, stars, sandpaper

So Lucky

Jennifer McCracken
Loveland, OH

*Supplies: Cardstock (Bazzill); patterned
paper, chipboard pieces (MAMBI); brads,
eyelet (BasicGrey); letters (Scenic Route);
ribbon (American Crafts); Misc: pen*

Beloved Little Boy

Nancy Doren
Colorado Springs, CO

*Supplies: Cardstock (Core'dinations);
patterned paper (Creative Imaginations,
My Little Yellow Bicycle, Déjà Views);
stickers (Making Memories, K&Co); letters
(American Crafts); epoxy sticker (K&Co);
Misc: paint, thread, ink, pen*

Play Mates

Terri Hayes
Cary, NC

Supplies: Cardstock (Bazzill); patterned paper (American Crafts, October Afternoon, My Little Shoebox); trim (Webster's Pages); stickers (American Crafts, BasicGrey, My Little Shoebox, October Afternoon); Misc: pen

Inspired Idea!

Once your child has outgrown a favorite blanket, outfit or pair of shoes, consider taking just a snip of it and using it on a layout. The page then serves as a reminder, allowing you to capture the memory but you don't have the bulk of storing everything she always loved. Being able to touch an actual snip of that special item will make your layout one to be treasured.

Blankie Love

Jamie Harder
Martensville, Saskatchewan

Supplies: Cardstock (Core'dinations); patterned paper, letters, journal spot (Jillibean Soup); chipboard hearts, buttons (Close To My Heart); Misc: brown pen, waxy floss, white acrylic paint

I Found Happiness

Terri Hayes
Cary, NC

Supplies: Patterned paper (Collage Press, Making Memories); rub-ons (Lily Bee); felt, crystals (Prima); stickers (Hambly, MAMBI); transparency (Little Yellow Bicycle); Misc: pen, chipboard

My Man Forever

Guiseppa Gubler
Wellsville, UT

Supplies: Cardstock (Bazzill); patterned paper (My Mind's Eye); letters (Adornit); brads (Sassafras Lass); flowers (Prima, BoBunny); adhesive foam (All Night Media); Misc: denim jeans

Our Love's the Only Truth

Renee' Morris-Dezember
Richland, WA

Supplies: Software (Photoshop 6.0); digital papers, scalloped border, stitching, digital letteres by CreativityByCrystal (Jessica Sprague, Two Peas in a Bucket); vintage stacked flowers by Kitschy Digitals (Jessica Sprague); zigzag stitches (Sande Kreiger)

True Love's Kiss

Michelle Kerrigan
Saint John, New Brunswick

Supplies: Cardstock (Prism); patterned paper (BoBunny); pearl swirls, lace (Prima); fabric button brad (BasicGrey); border punch (Martha Stewart Crafts), glitter mist (Tattered Angels), shimmer font sticker (Making Memories); ink (Ranger); Misc: circle punch, thread, Hand Writing font by Ali Edwards, pink circle font (Pink Paisley)

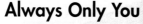

Always Only You

April Derrick
Hot Spring Village, AR

Supplies: Cardstock (Bazzill); patterned paper (Fancy Pants); letters (Cosmo Cricket, American Crafts); stickers (Heidi Swapp); rub-ons (BasicGrey); pin (Fancy Pants); silver tape (Magic Mesh); metal clips (7gypsies); canvas frame (Making Memories); 3D Flower (KI Memories); Misc: black pen, glitter, mini-staples, colored pencils, metallic acrylic paint, color wash

I Love U

Loredana Bucaria
Quarto Napoli, Italy

Supplies: Cardstock (Bazzill); patterned paper, chipboard pieces, letters (American Crafts); Misc: brown gel pen, punches

Lovebirds

Kristen Jo Simmons
Milton, KY

Supplies: Cardstock (Bazzill); patterned paper, chipboard embellishments, stickers (Crate Paper); letters (American Crafts); rub-ons (Hambly); Misc: pen

Inspired Idea!

It's a little thing, but the torn edges on this layout go a long way. Simply make a small tear along the outside of your layout and use sandpaper to rough it up. Adhere a coordinating pattern behind it and allow that bit of color to pop. If you do this, it's best to do it in an odd number of spots. The tears then create a lovely visual triangle that perfectly guides the eye around the page.

Piece of My Heart

Katie Burnett
Birmingham, AL

Supplies: Patterned paper (Bella Blvd, Jenni Bowlin, Lily Bee, Making Memories); letters (Pink Paislee, October Afternoon); glitter chipboard (American Crafts); glitter glue (Ranger); charm (Scripts Kit); stickers (Sassafras Lass); Misc: twine, key, heart puzzle, pen

Still the One

Jennifer Day
Ottawa, Ontario

Supplies: Cardstock (Bazzill); patterned paper (Little Yellow Bicycle, Making Memories, My Mind's Eye); chipboard frame, tag (MAMBI); letters (Colorbök, Making Memories, Scenic Route); bling (Prima, Recollections); transparency (7gypsies); ribbon (Close To My Heart); photo corners (Martha Stewart Crafts); journaling card (My Mind's Eye); Misc: ink, punch, twine, Jenni Bowlin packaging

Love Letter

Amy Wilhelms
Medford, OR

Supplies: Cardstock (Bazzill); patterned paper (Fiskars, Creative Imaginations); die-cut paper (Autumn Leaves); die-cut stickers (Creative Imaginations); die-cut shape (Fiskars); chipboard (Heidi Swapp); flowers (Prima, Bazzill); letters (American Crafts, Webster's Pages); lace trim (Prima); rub-on (7gypsies); distress ink (Ranger); Misc: floss, ink, brad, decorative scissors, Colonna MT font

Inspired Idea!

Some of the coolest embellishments aren't made for scrapbooking—they're made for clothing! Shoes, clothes and even a slogan button pin make up the embellishments for this layout, and they are the perfect complement to the photos and design! Keep a special envelope or box for found items like these tags—you never know when they're going to perfectly mesh with your intended design!

Love of a Lifetime

Staci Etheridge
(Memory Makers Master, 2008)
McKinney, TX

Supplies: Patterned paper (Sassafras Lass); ink (Clearsnap); label die-cut (Collage Press); ribbon (Webster's Pages); Misc: acrylic paint, clothing tags, badge pin

Inspired Idea!

Patterned paper isn't so sacred it can't be run through a printer! Don't hesitate to print your journaling, or even the lyrics to your favorite song, right on the background of your page. Yes, you've got a pattern to compete with, but the result can be interesting to look at, fun to read and the perfect way to show off a meaningful photo you're sure to love.

Just Love Me

Brianne Nevill
Fort Lewis, WA

Supplies: Patterned paper, tab (October Afternoon); chipboard heart (Rusty Pickle); notebook paper (Making Memories); letters (Pink Paislee, American Crafts); adhesive (3M, Plaid, Helmar); Misc: paper clip, twine, ink, distressing tool, pen, CK Good Day font

Thank You

Ellen Sosnoski
Paxinos, PA

Supplies: Cardstock (Bazzill); patterned paper, felt flowers, letters (Jillibean Soup); digital frame by Rhonna Farrer (Two Peas in a Bucket); date stamp (Heidi Swapp); adhesive (Helmar); Misc: floss, ink, Glossy Accents Puget font (Chatterbox)

i can't believe my little baby is a toddler now. Two years old, my girl is growing up
July 26, 2008

Chapter Five:

KIDS, BABIES AND PETS

A large portion of our scrapbook albums consist of pages about kids and pets. They are, after all, two of the most important aspects of our lives. Once you start a family, you undoubtedly need ideas on how to scrapbook them—and you need look no further than this chapter.

Chock-full of inspiration, this chapter hits every emotion you feel thanks to those little bundles of joy. The sweet bliss of the newborn baby, the challenging teaching times with a toddler, even the simple moment where you sit back and realize how blessed your life is because of the tiny people who are in it. You'll find it all right here.

And of course, no family album would be complete without a page or two on man's best friend—or feline. Pets truly are part of the family, and the ideas you'll find on the following pages will inspire you to make them a part of your albums as well!

First Day

Caroline Rondel
Haucourt, France

*Supplies: Paper (La Compagnie du Kraft);
watercolor paint (Pelikan); gesso (Lefranc
& Bourgeois); Misc: paper doily, tracing
paper, brush printed onto transparency,
tag, sewing thread, tulle, staples*

Inspired Idea!

Using several different embellishments on a layout can be intimidating, but not if you take Iris' advice! In order to keep the embellishments in check, she established borders for her layout. The ruler at the bottom and the large photo corner in the upper right-hand corner keep everything locked in together and provide the perfect little area for all kinds of fun goodies!

My Beautiful Baby

Iris Babao Uy
(Memory Makers Master, 2008)
Quezon City, Metro Manila, Philippines

*Supplies: Patterned paper (7gypsies,
Memory Box), flowers, flower center, twill
(Prima), rub-ons (Lily Bee, Hambly), chip-
board (Provo Craft)*

One Month

Nicole Stark
(Memory Makers Master, 2007)
Roy, UT

Supplies: Cardstock (Bazzill); patterned paper (Crate Paper, Studio Calico, Cosmo Cricket); letters, labels (Jenni Bowlin); die-cut circles, chipboard (Sassafras Lass); die-cut star (Provo Craft); pen (American Crafts)

First Diaper

Meg Barker
Detroit Lakes, MN

Supplies: Patterned paper (October Afternoon); chipboard accent (My Mind's Eye); journaling block (Luxe designs); letters (American Crafts); overlays (Hambly); trim (Bazzill); Misc: pen, stickers, fabric

This is you

Jennifer Day
Ottawa, Ontario

Supplies: Cardstock (Bazzill); patterned paper (Pink Paislee); letters (American Crafts, Making Memories); stamp (Close To My Heart); Misc: ink, punch, floss

10 Months

Meg Barker
Detroit Lakes, MN

Supplies: Cardstock (Bazzill); journaling cards (Little Yellow Bicycle); letters (American Crafts); stickers (Heidi Grace); Misc: pen, fabric, mesh

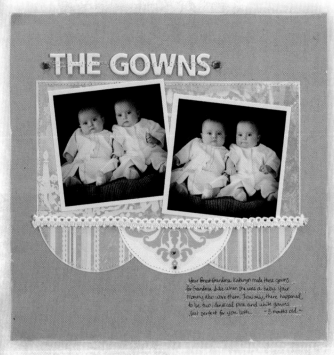

The Gowns

Jill Cornell
Windsor Heights, IA

Supplies: Cardstock (Bazzill); patterned paper, rhinestones, lace trim (Melissa Frances); chipboard letters (BasicGrey); sticker (Heidi Swapp); Misc: thread, acrylic paint

18 Months

Yvette Adams
Banks, Australia

Supplies: Patterned paper (Scenic Route, Crate Paper); letters (American Crafts); journaling notepaper (Making Memories); embossing powder (American Crafts); trims (Doodlebug); brads (Creative Imaginations, Doodlebug); Misc: chipboard, fabric, pen, dressmakers pattern, circle punch

You're my Tootsie Wootsie

Becky Teichmiller
Mukwonago, WI

Supplies: Patterned paper (October Afternoon); buttons (BasicGrey); brads (Queen & Co); lollipop, flower (Prima); pearls (Kaisercraft); letters (Provo Craft, Making Memories); Misc: adhesive

Erin

Elaine Hunter
Houston, Scotland

Supplies: Cardstock (Bazzill); patterned paper (Cosmo Cricket); ribbon, crochet flower (American Crafts); stickers, journal block (Sassafras Lass); clear rhinestone gems (Hero Arts); ink (Stampin' Up!); foam ink applicator (Ranger); Misc: pen, punch, scissors, sewing machine, white thread

Whoo Loves You?

Sarah Eclavea
Oswego, IL

Supplies: Cardstock (BoBunny, Bazzill); patterned paper (Jillibean Soup, TPC Studios); letters (American Crafts); stickers (BasicGrey); chipboard (BasicGrey, Heidi Grace); Misc: ink, punch, label maker

Baby in Action

Juliet Adora Concepcion
Renton, WA

Supplies: Patterned paper (BasicGrey, Sassafras Lass); letters, buttons (Making Memories); stickers (Cosmo Cricket)

Wild Thing

Jan Barlow
Muncy, PA

Supplies: Cardstock (DCWV); patterned paper (Sassafras Lass); flower tag (Nicole Crafts); die-cutting machine (Making Memories); flower punches, precision scissors (EK Success); white ink pen (Uniball); Misc: adhesive, ink, floss, sequin, flower brad, swirl clip, edge-cutting scissors, ribbon, adhesive crystals

Celebrate Time With You

April Derrick
Hot Spring Village, AR

Supplies: Cardstock (Prism); patterned paper (We R Memory Keepers); transparency (Hambly); letters (American Crafts); stickers (Heidi Swapp, Making Memories); rub-ons (BasicGrey, Maya Road, Daisy D's, Luxe); plastic tab (Heidi Swapp); software (Adobe PSE 6); digital paper (Stacey Towers); digital staple by Keyr Arun (Dreams Inspired); digital number stamp (Sueli Colbert Designs); Misc: pens, glitter, rhinestone, black notebook paper, washi tape, mini staples

Handmade with Love

Leilani Pamplona Villegas
Antioch, CA

Supplies: Cardstock (Close To My Heart); patterned paper (My Mind's Eye); letters (Li'l Davis); chipboard hearts (Heidi Grace); flowers (Heidi Swapp), word (K&Co); Misc: buttons, marker

Inspired Idea

Sure you could throw away those index-print sized photos, but why not use them instead? Once you've selected your larger photos, scan the index card for runners-up that didn't quite make the enlargement cut. Cut them out and use them to decorate your embellishments for a uniquely personal touch.

Bubbles

Melanie Smith
Conception Bay South, Newfoundland

Supplies: Cardstock (Bazzill); letters (Maya Road); stamps (Hero Arts); Misc: flower

Mobile

Bethany Kartchner
Laveen, AZ

Supplies: Cardstock (Bazzill); patterned paper: (Pink Paislee, BasicGrey, Scenic Route, KI Memories, GCD Studios); overlay (Luxe); chipboard sign, buttons (GCD Studios); clown hat clipart (Tangie Baxter); brads (7gypsies); chipboard star (Cosmo Cricket); paint (Shimmerz); Misc: pen, acrylic paint, rick rack, staples, sequin waste, colored pencils, fabric

Joy and Strength

Katherine Blue
Elkridge, MD

Supplies: Patterned paper (Creative Imaginations, K&Co); trim (GCD Studios); brad (Doodlebug); gemstones (Hero Arts); letters (American Crafts, BasicGrey); mini-accents (K&Co); pen (Uniball); spray ink (Clearsnap); Misc: sewing trims, pin, pen, epoxy

My Littlest Guy

Julie Gordon
Carramar, Australia

Supplies: Cardstock (Bazzill); patterned paper, letters (BasicGrey); stickers (Making Memories); brads (Kaisercraft, Making Memories); Misc: thread, pens, buttons

Your World

Guiseppa Gubler
Wellsville, UT

*Supplies: Cardstock (Bazzill); patterned
paper (My Mind's Eye, Crate Paper, SEI);
leather frame (All My Memories);
rub-ons (October Afternoon);
adhesive foam (All Night Media);
letters (Li'l Davis); Misc: Garamond font*

Adorable Makeup Girl

Heather Carpenter
Baton Rouge, LA

*Supplies: Cardstock (Bazzill); patterned paper, chipboard accent, rub-ons, ribbon (Imaginisce); letters (Cosmo Cricket); border punch
(Fiskars); Misc: adhesive, Garamond font*

Spotlight On...

Summer Fullerton
Tigard, OR

Summer Fullerton
is the coauthor of *Remember This*. With 120 fresh layout ideas, *Remember This* will inspire you to scrap a variety of creative layouts during every season of the year. With pages featuring multiple photos, numerous styles and a variety of events and activities there's something for every scrapper.

Pre-K

Supplies: Cardstock (Bazzill); specialty paper (Core'dinations, Jillibean Soup); patterned paper, letters, shipping tag (Jillibean Soup); rhinestones (Doodlebug); buttons, month rub-on (Jenni Bowlin); stamp (Unity); punch (Stampin' Up); caption maker (Dymo); Misc: vellum, ink, pencil, foam squares, floss, Bohemian Typewriter font

Little Scorekeeper

Supplies: Cardstock (Bazzill); specialty paper (Core'dinations, Jillibean Soup); patterned paper, letters (Jillibean Soup); punch (Fiskars); pearl brad (American Crafts); metal accent (We R Memory Keepers); Misc: buttons, floss, felt, Bohemian Typewriter font

Alexa at 8

Ali Lacher
Bloomington, MN

Supplies: Cardstock (Bazzill); patterned paper, letters, stickers, chipboard (BasicGrey)

Inspired Idea!

If you like to photograph your child at each stage (on or near his/her birthday), why not break away from the traditional posed portrait and capture them where they are happiest? For these photos, Ali wanted to shoot her daughter on the playground, one of her favorite places at age eight. Not only does this provide a fun setting for a shoot, it also adds to the memory of her daughter at this stage.

Little Bathing Beauty

Victoria Murray
Toronto, Ontario

Supplies: Cardstock (Prism); patterned paper (Graphic 45); letters (October Afternoon); felt flourish, flowers (Prima); rhinestones, pearls (Kaisercraft); picture frame (House of Three); software (Adobe)

Tiny Hands

Becky Williams
Wolfforth, TX

Supplies: Patterned paper, chipboard, journal spot (Cosmo Cricket); pearls (Prima, Zva Creative); lace trim (Prima); buttons (Creative Imaginations)

Bloom

Amy Martin
(Memory Makers Master, 2009)
Corpus Christi, TX

Supplies: Software (Corel PaintShopPro vXl); letters, brad (Jenni Bowlin); stamps (October Afternoon); Misc: Thread, Kenner Road Kit, Maszyna Royal Dark font

Animated

Sandi Minchuk
Merrillville, IN

Supplies: Cardstock (Bazzill); patterned paper (Crate Paper, K&Co, SEI); button (SEI); chipboard pieces (Maya Road); flower (Prima); letters (American Crafts); photo mat (Creative Memories); Misc: pen, thread, edge distresser, glass beads, machine stitching, adhesive

Attitude is in da House

Stephanie Garbett
Stourbridge, England

Supplies: Cardstock (Bazzill); patterned papers (Webster's Pages); flowers, brads, stamp (Prima); Misc: gel pens, punches

Facts of Five

Dana E. Tate
Saint Clair, MO

Supplies: Software (Adobe Photoshop CS3); papers, digital elements (Zoe Pearn)

Inspired Idea!

Love the look of studio portraits but hate the portrait prices? Why not try your hand at shooting a few of your own? Simply set up a solid sheet for the background and position your subject in a spot where there is excellent natural light. Experiment with your camera's settings and even change up the background colors for a variety of different portraits…for free!

Be Happy

Star Rork
Saunemin, IL

Supplies: Patterned paper (Provo Craft, My Mind's Eye); brads (Making Memories, The Paper Studio); flowers (The Paper Studio); stickers (Adornit, October Afternoon); Misc: scissors, marker, trimmer, scallop scissors

Three

Katie Burnett
Birmingham, AL

Supplies: Cardstock (Martha Stewart Crafts); patterned paper (SEI, Lily Bee, Provo Craft); letters (American Crafts); brads (BasicGrey, Autumn Leaves); charm (Tim Holtz/Advantus); Misc: punches, adhesive

Capturing the Moment

Ria Mojica
Pasig, Metro Manila, Philppines

Supplies: Cardstock (KI Memories); patterned paper (Pink Paislee, SEI); sticker (Jenni Bowlin); rub-ons (Daisy D's); Misc: pen

It's The Little Things

Heather Bowser
Brandon, MS

Supplies: Cardstock (Core'dinations); brads (Stampin' Up); ink (Versamark); embossing powder (American Crafts); die-cut machines (Silhouette, Sizzix); embossing folder (Provo Craft)

Always & Forever

Christyn Holmes
Littleton, CO

Supplies: Patterned paper (Sassafras Lass, Studio Calico, Cosmo Cricket, My Mind's Eye); flash card (7gypsies); letters (Harmonie); stamp (Studio Calico); ribbon (American Crafts), flower (Prima); sticker (GCD Studio); Misc: buttons, ink, doily

Cookie Mama

Connie Hyde Mercer
Belmont, TX

Supplies: Patterned paper (BasicGrey, Making Memories); felt woolies (BasicGrey); letters (American Crafts); chipboard (Scenic Route); Misc: pen, border punch, rhinestones

Inspired Idea!

Elements printed onto patterned paper make the greatest embellishments when cut out and repurposed. For this page, Deana cut out the clouds and sunflower to create her own summer scene. Topped off with two rows of fringy grass, you can almost feel the heat of the summer sun when you look at this page!

Bee Happy

Deana Boston
O'Fallon, MO

Supplies: Cardstock (Recollections); patterned paper, craft flag, stamps (Nikki Sivils); letters (American Crafts, Nikki Sivils packaging); Misc: pen, thread, SNF Little Star Sketch

It's a Girl Thing

Liana Suwandi
Wylie, TX

Supplies: Cardstock (Bazzill); Patterned paper, mini tags, stickers, tranparency, rub-ons (Fancy Pants); swirl glitter rub-ons (We R Memory Keepers); felt flower, jewel (Little Yellow Bicycle); heart throbs (Queen & Co); butterfly punch (Martha Stewart Crafts); border punch (Fiskar); paper cutter (Purple Cows)

Warning to all Future Suitors

Wendy Kwok
Singapore

Supplies: Patterned paper (Anna Griffin, Graphic 45); flowers (Prima); pearls (Jenni Bowlin); letters (American Crafts); stickers (7gypsies, My Little Shoebox); tag (Elle's Studio)

KC

Brooke Clark
Simi Valley, CA

Supplies: Cardstock (Bazzill); patterned paper (My Mind's Eye, Sassafras Lass, Studio Calico); chipboard (Sassafras Lass packaging); letters, buttons (American Crafts); sticker (Sassafras Lass); jewels (Prima); film strip (Ranger); rub-ons (Hambly); Misc: pen

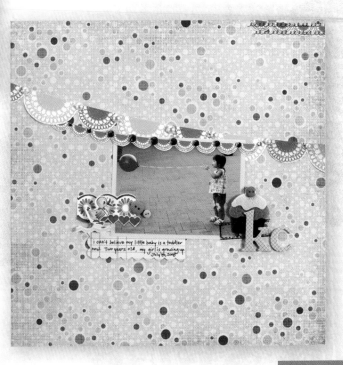

A Loopy Kind of Girl

Jing-Jing Nickel
Roseville, MN

Supplies: Patterned paper (Lily Bee); stickers (SRM, 7gypsies); letters (American Crafts, BasicGrey, My Little Shoebox); punch (Martha Stewart Crafts, Fiskars); pen (American Crafts)

Aren't They Loverly

Michelle Houghton
Clive, IA

Supplies: Cardstock (Bazzill, Archiver's); letters, flowers, bird (BasicGrey); sticker letters (Pioneer); Misc: pen, floss

Be Silly

Jennifer Wuthrich
Evans, CO

Supplies: Cardstock (Bazzill); patterned paper (BasicGrey); letters (Pressed Petals, BasicGrey); floral stickers (BasicGrey); ribbon (Offray); Misc: Santa's Sleigh font

Fairy Tales

Stephanie Eaken
Richmond, VA

Supplies: Cardstock (Bazzill); patterned paper (My Mind's Eye, BasicGrey); chipboard clock (Making Memories); pink letters (American Crafts); blue and black letters (October Afternoon); Misc: butterfly punch, scallop punch, brad, pearl

That Girl

Muriel Croom
Chula Vista, CA

Supplies: Cardstock (Bazzill); patterned paper (My Mind's Eye); stamp (Imaginisce); rhinestone (Studio 18); digital graphics (Silhouette); photo editing software (Picnik); Misc: colored pencil, punch

Beyond Bored

Jill Sarginson
Kanata, Ontario

Supplies: Cardstock (Bazzill); patterned paper (My Mind's Eye, Scenic Route); letters (Bazzill, BasicGrey); border punches (Fiskars); Misc: Century Gothic font

Inspired Idea!

Corrugated cardboard isn't just for moving boxes and storage! A rectangle of this funky stuff serves as a great photo mat for a focal point photo that needs an added punch. Like foam dots, corrugated cardboard will pop an element off the page, drawing the eye right to it in a flash. It also adds a grungy, handmade look that's extra fun.

Upside Down Shades

Lynn Y. Kopas
North Attleboro, MA

Supplies: Patterned paper (Scenic Route, My Mind's Eye, Creative Imaginations, Jenni Bowlin); letters (American Crafts, BasicGrey, Making Memories); journaling strips (Jenni Bowlin); ink (Clearsnap); Misc: buttons, brad, staples, jute, stickles, corrugated cardboard, black pen

Wacky Hair Day

Bethany Kartchner
Laveen, AZ

Supplies: Cardstock (Bazzill); patterned paper (Scenic Route, BoBunny); rub-ons (Luxe); jewels (Fashion Jewels); butterfly (Heidi Swapp/Advantus); stamps (Imaginesce, Fontwerks); Misc: pen, colored pencils, ink, scissors

Yuck!

Ilene Tell
Wilmington, DE

Supplies: Patterned paper, stickers (Sassafras Lass); letters (Doodlebug, Making Memories); journaling spot (Making Memories); rub-ons (BasicGrey); Misc: ink

Why?

Diana Brodeur
Lawton, OK

Supplies: Cardstock (American Crafts); patterned paper, stamp (Studio Calico); glitter mist (Maya Road); ink (StazOn); floss (DMC)

Will Sign for Food

Gina Johnson
Mt. Carmel, IL

Supplies: Cardstock (Bazzill); patterned paper (BasicGrey, We R Memory Keepers); letters (American Crafts, Jenni Bowlin, My Little Shoebox); mist (Tattered Angels); pearls (Kaisercraft); Misc: floss, ink, marker, three heart punch, eyelet border punch, modern label punch, pen

Inspired Idea!

If you've got stamps and aren't quite sure what else to do with them, look no further than the paper flowers in your stash. The stamped designs add a neat effect and breathe new life into the otherwise plain flowers. For added interest, spray them with Shimmerz Spritz. You've just reinvented the flowers and gotten great use out of your stamps!

Sweet

Stacy Cohen
Los Angeles, CA

Supplies: Cardstock (Bazzill); patterned paper (October Afternoon); letters (American Crafts); flowers, gems (Prima); tag (Making Memories); glitter mist (Shimmerz); Misc: ink, jute, dimensional gloss medium, buttons

From the day you were born you have always had such a sweet disposition. I wondered if you were going to go through a not-so-easy phase like some kids do, but luckily that hasn't happened. At age 5 you are sweeter than ever. You are such a kind-hearted little girl!

Thankful For

Vicki Flinchum
Round Rock, TX

Supplies: Patterned paper (Kaisercraft); buttons (Rusty Pickle); rub-ons (Piggy Tales); software (Adobe Photoshop Elements 2.0); acrylic paint (Ranger); glitter mist (Tattered Angels); Misc: ink, embossing powder, floss, crinoline, empty jar

Things You Say

Robyn Schaub
Dallas, TX

Supplies: Cardstock (Bazzill); patterned paper (American Crafts, Pink Paislee); chipboard frames (American Crafts); letters (QuickKutz); die-cut shapes (QuickKutz, Making Memories); metal flower (Making Memories); Misc: pen, seam binding, adhesive, embroidery floss

This Moment

Jill Paulson
Yankton, SD

Supplies: Cardstock (Bazzill); patterned paper (BoBunny); rub-ons (BasicGrey, Fancy Pants); chipboard (Pebbles); pins, rick rack (Making Memories); ink (Clearsnap); Misc: Floral Dawn font, Capture It 2 font, American Typewriter font

Inspired Idea!

When your mojo is on vacation, you don't have to avoid your scraproom altogether! If you're having trouble getting started, why not turn to a sketch or even "scraplift" one of your own layouts? You can flip it around, change up the color scheme and you'll have an entirely new layout to fall in love with.

The Clown

Kay Rogers
Midland, MI

Supplies: Cardstock (Bazzill); patterned paper, stickers, chipboard accents (BasicGrey); Misc: corner punch, pen

Just A Simple Shoot

Romy Veul
Uithoorn, Netherlands

Supplies: Patterned paper (My Mind's Eye); crystal corner, flower, pearls (Prima); letters (American Crafts, Kaisercraft); rub-ons (Kaisercraft); edge distresser (Heidi Swapp); Misc: black marker, white pen, punch, scissors, glitter, ink

Hang On

Beth Hallgren
Hartford, MI

Supplies: Cardstock (Bazzill); patterned paper (BasicGrey); letter stickers (American Crafts); gems (MAMBI); punch (We R Memory Keepers); Misc: floss, chipboard circles, adhesive, Lucinda Handwriting font

Inspired Idea!

When your photos speak for themselves, there's really no need to go overboard on the design aspect of your layout. Instead, add a few key elements to ground the pictures and you've really set up those special pictures to shine! An additional cluster of words and decoration near the bottom gives you a chance to include a special message without distracting from the focal point of the page.

Kristen

Carol Monson
Las Vegas, NV

Supplies: Cardstock (Bazzill); patterned paper (Sassafras Lass, Cosmo Cricket, Studio Calico); chipboard, glitter mist (Maya Road); ribbon, vinyl (American Crafts); letters (BasicGrey); stamp (Studio Calico); Misc: baker's twine, ink, pen

Beauty

Katherine Blue
Elkridge, MD

Supplies: Patterned paper (My Mind's Eye); border, rub-ons (K&Co); brads (Colorbök); letters (American Crafts); ribbon (Fancy Pants); stickpin (Making Memories); writer (EK Success); Misc: sewing trims, tulle, thread, epoxy

Growing Up

Laura Achilles
Littleton, CO

Supplies: Cardstock (Bazzill); patterned paper (7gypsies, BasicGrey, Crate Paper); letters (American Crafts, My Little Shoebox); brad (BasicGrey); rub-ons (Crate Paper); glitter mist (Tattered Angels); template (Crafters Workshop); Misc: pen, ink, adhesive, vintage tape measure

Sparkle

Chrissy Joester
Queensland, Australia

Supplies: Cardstock (Bazzill); patterned paper (Kaisercraft); letters (American Craft); flowers (Green Tara); ribbon (Birch, Vandoros); pearl strips (Kaisercraft); heart mirror (Heidi Swapp); Misc: chipboard flourish, plastic brad, Monotype Corsiva font

Spotlight On...

Lisa M. Pace
Frisco, TX

Lisa M. Pace
is the author of *Delight in the Details*. Inside the book, learn how to create unique accents with a variety of materials, from simple paper and fabric scraps to glitter, ink, modeling paste and vintage finds. One hundred lovely projects—including greeting cards, scrapbook layouts, mini albums and home décor—showcase the techniques in fabulous form. Visit Lisa at www.lisapace.com.

Sweet 16

Supplies: Patterned paper, stickers, buttons, butterfly, memo pad (Jenni Bowlin); pearls (The Paper Studio); punch (Martha Stewart Crafts); ink (Clearsnap); decorative scissors (Fiskars); Misc: baker's twine, rhinestone, seam binding

Love

Supplies: Patterned paper, stickers, butterfly (Jenni Bowlin), pearls (The Paper Studio); glitter (Ranger); pearlescent chalks (Pebbles); card (DCWV); ink (Clearsnap); decorative scissors (Fiskars); Misc: baker's twine, flower, adhesive

Imagine

Kirsten Peverelle
Shawnigan Lake, British Columbia

Supplies: Cardstock (Bazzill); patterned paper (BasicGrey); letters (Adornit); pen (American Crafts)

Inspired Idea!

Sometimes it seems we have to stay serious in our scrapbooks. But don't forget the humor that fills your every day. Taking a comical approach gives you a different kind of memory and puts things in a light that makes even the most trying times something to laugh about.

Super Tantrum

Sara Peterson
Albany, OR

Supplies: Software (Adobe Photoshop CS4); software script by Christy Vanderwall (Rename Layers); digital paper, digital frame, digital journal paper, digital arrow, digital letters by Angie Briggs (Scrap Girls); digital photoshop brush by Brandie Valenzuela (Scrap Girls); digital stitching by Amanda McGee (Scrap Girls); Misc: Eccentric font, LD Squirrel Tracks font

100% Boy

Mireille Divjak
Den Helder, Holland

Supplies: Cardstock (Bazzill); patterned paper, die-cut (My Mind's Eye); stamps (Recollections); Misc: pen, acrylic paint, punch, ink, figure scissors, magic mesh

Achievements

Katharyn Brine
Murrumbateman, Australia

Supplies: Software (Adobe Photosop Elements 6); cardstock, flourish by Anna Aspnes (Designer Digitals); stitching border by Ali Edwards (Designer Digitals); tied heart by CS (unknown); patterned paper by Michelle Martin (Designer Digitals); letters by Katie Pertiet, Mindy Terasawa, Rob & Bob Studio, Lynne Grieveson, Anna Aspnes, Pattie Knox (Designer Digitals), letters by Miss Mint (Peppermint Creative)

My Wish

Amy Martin
(Memory Makers Master, 2009)
Corpus Christi, TX

Supplies: Software (Corel PaintShopPro vXI); letters (American Crafts); stickers (Jenni Bowlin); Misc: cardboard, vintage ribbon, sticker stars, Kenner Road Kit, CK Classical font

Inspired Idea!

It's easy to shy away from using flowers on your boy layouts, but don't! They add a soft, natural touch that isn't only reserved for feminine layouts. This page is a wonderful tribute to a sweet little boy—and because it's well designed, it's the photo you notice, not the fact that there are flowers outlining a boy's picture!

Always

Julie Gordon
Carramar, Australia

Supplies: Cardstock (Bazzill); patterned paper (Crate Paper); letters (BasicGrey); chipboard (Cosmo Cricket); pearls (Prima); trinket pin (Maya Road); Misc: ribbon, punches

An Angel Among Us

Guiseppa Gubler
Wellsville, UT

Supplies: Cardstock (Bazzill); patterned paper (October Afternoon, My Mind's Eye, Making Memories); chipboard (Fancy Pants, K&Co); felt branch (Prima); letters (Adornit); rub-ons (October Afternoon, Pink Paislee); Misc: Lainie Day font, Agency font

Born to be a Rock Star

Julia Krause
Reutlingen, Germany

Supplies: Cardstock (Core'dinations; patterned paper (My Mind's Eye, Sassafras Lass); letters (American Crafts, Doodlebug, Making Memories); embellishments (My Mind's Eye, BasicGrey, Fancy Pants, BoBunny); Misc: ink, punch, sewing machine, Wacky Action BTN font

Boy's Charm

Emeline Seet
Singapore

Supplies: Cardstock (Bazzill); patterned paper, chipboard, vintage resin appliqués (Melissa Frances); pearls (Melissa Frances, Prima); Misc: buttons, ink, butterfly punch, pin

Inspired Idea!

Don't be afraid to use ink right on the edges of your photos. This will give the pictures a somewhat distressed feel, but it will also help pop them off the layout, instantly making them the focal point of the page. If the ink doesn't dry right away, a quick shot with an embossing gun should do the trick!

Can I Keep It

Jackie Weeks
Ft. Pierce, FL

Supplies: Cardstock (Bazzill); patterned paper, cardstock stickers (Sassafras Lass); letters (My Little Shoebox); Misc: acrylic paint, buttons

Apples of my Eye

Jennifer Day
Ottawa, Ontario

Supplies: Cardstock (Bazzill); patterned paper (October Afternoon, Making Memories, My Mind's Eye); chipboard (BasicGrey); letters, hatpin (Making Memories); pearls (Recollections); die-cut (Stampin' Up!); punch (Fiskars); Misc: ink, floss

Is There an Echo in Here?

Jennifer Day
Ottawa, Ontario

Supplies: Cardstock (Bazzill); letters, chipboard border (Making Memories); transparency (Little Yellow Bicycle); felt stars (Close To My Heart); Misc: ink, Lucida Sans Typewriter font

Extra! Extra!

KIDS • PETS • TEENS

These layouts show how you can get inspired by a layout with any subject! Use a layout you love, but make your own photos the star. The two layouts on the next page were both inspired by the layout below.

DEC 07

Micah you truely are a star

that shines, with your cheeky grins

and your eyes full of mischeif.

YOU ARE A
★ STAR
BRIGHT SHINING
TWINKLE IN MY EYE

You Are a Star

Janine Worthington
Whangarei, New Zealand

Supplies: Patterned paper (BasicGrey, Fancy Pants); embellishments (My Mind's Eye, Jenni Bowlin); Misc: acrylic paint, staples, date stamp, old typewriter

Our Little Princess

after much debate we agreed on a name. This new dog will be named princess. ♡

Miss Princess

May Flaum
Vacaville, CA

Supplies: Patterned paper, stamp, chipboard label (Teresa Collins); chipboard letters (Pink Paislee); ribbon (May Arts); digital patterned papers by Katie Pertiet (Designer Digitals); digital journaling label by Ali Edwards (Designer Digitals); felt circle embellishment (Evalicious); pin (Maya Road); butterfly (Jenni Bowlin); flower (Prima); brad (American Crafts); ink (StazOn); Misc: thread, buttons, rhinestone accent

MAR 2010

Lexi you are fiesty, spirited a bit sassy, independent with just the right amount of sweetness

More Spice Than Sugar

More Spice Than Sugar

Ronda Palazzari
(Memory Makers Master, 2009)
Thornton, CO

Supplies: Cardstock (Bazzill); patterned paper, rub-ons, glitter die-cuts, ribbon (Fancy Pants); stamp (Purple Onion); Misc: paint, walnut ink, typewriter, ink

Where's the Beef?

Rochelle Spears
Anaheim, CA

Supplies: Cardstock, buttons (Bazzill); patterned paper (Fancy Pants); letters (American Craft); chipboard (Making Memories); tickets (Jenni Bowlin); Misc: pen, decorative scissors, punch, staples, distresser, embossing powder, ink

He's a Heartbreaker

Tiff Sawyer
Camden, Australia

Supplies: Cardstock (Core'dination'); patterned paper (My Mind's Eye, Kaisercraft, 7gypsies); chipboard wings, chipboard heart (Bella Blvd.); decorative clip (K&Co); chipboard clock (CherryArte); bull nose clip, small metal clip (Making Memories); die-cut arrow (Scenic Route); letters (American Crafts); mounted stamp (Stampin' Up); Misc: handmade paper strip, staples, ink, paint, black felt pen

Inspired Idea!

Oversized frames are a great addition to any page, and if you cut them apart you get them to pull double duty! This frame became a completely different element when Isabel positioned it on either side of her photo. Don't be afraid to alter something and use it in a different way than it was originally intended. The results might be just what you're looking for!

Beau Nageur

Isabel Do Nascimento
Houilles, France

Supplies: Patterned paper (Heidi Grace); chipboard label frame (Jenni Bowlin); sticker (Sassafras Lass); letters (Pink Paislee); Misc: rub-on, pen

It Happens

Lydia Jackson
Merville, British Columbia

Supplies: Patterned paper, stickers, ribbon, date circle (Jillibean Soup); buttons (Jilibean Soup, Foof a la)

All Star Kids

Jessica Jo Salber
Wausau, WI

Supplies: Cardstock (Bazzill); patterned paper (Scenic Route, Jenni Bowlin); letters (BasicGrey); chipboard star (Maya Road); Misc: pen, paint, brads, flag, fabric strip

Inspired Idea!

It's tempting to only use the most beautiful photos in your scrapbook albums, but resist that temptation! If you don't, you'll end up with albums that don't represent real life—and don't really mean that much to you. These simple, everyday photos may not seem like anything special, but someday, when Katherine looks back at it, she'll remember instantly the special stuffed friend her son carried with him. Don't neglect the little things!

Meet Mack

Katherine Blue
Elkridge, MD

Supplies: Cardstock (Bazzill); patterned paper (Provo Craft); brads (Imaginisce); chipboard (Colorbök, Making Memories); die-cut (My Mind's Eye); filmstrip (Tim Holtz); journaling spot (Jenni Bowlin); letters (American Crafts); Misc: thread, sewing trim, edged scissors, stickers

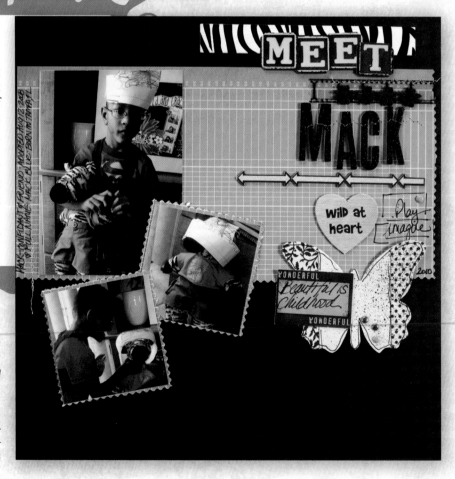

Oops!

Lisa Webb
Kawana Island, Queensland, Australia

Supplies: Patterned paper (Kaisercraft, Fancy Pants, My Mind's Eye); journal tag (My Mind's Eye); floss (Jenni Bowlin); chipboard bird (Provo Craft); Misc: button, felt, thread

Crimson & Blue

Amanda Schurman-Chard
Olathe, KS

Supplies: Cardstock (The Paper Studio); chipboard shapes, rub-ons (Making Memories); Misc: pen, punch, ink

Smiles

Tricia Gorden
South Bend, IN

Supplies: Cardstock (Bazzill); patterned paper (Scrap Within Reach); chipboard pieces (Technique Tuesday, Scenic Route); pearls (Kaisercraft); flower (Petaloo); letters (Adornit); Misc: pen, floss, ink, glitter spray, embossing folder

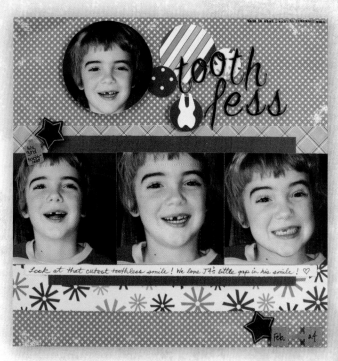

Toothless

Bonnie Fechter
Wyoming, MN

Supplies: Cardstock (DCWV); patterned papers (Scenic Route, Making Memories); letters, white pen (American Crafts); clear stamps by Ali Edwards (Technique Tuesday); Misc: punches, pen, adhesive foam

It's a Comfort Thing

Kim Holmes
Mountlake Terrace, WA

Supplies: Patterned paper (Fancy Pants, Adornit, BasicGrey); letters (Sassafras Lass, Adornit); chipboard (Bazzill); Misc: punch, thread, buttons, adhesive

It's A Wonderful World

Marita Waldner
Macgregor, MB

Supplies: Cardstock (unknown); patterned paper (K&Co); Misc: string, metal embellishments, Courier New font

Inspired Idea!

The oversized circle in this layout is the perfect focal point to this page—and it wasn't difficult to create. In Microsoft Publisher, simply create a circle shape, then insert the photo and journaling. Print onto cardstock for a textured feel and cut it out! This is a simple, easy way to liven up your layout!

Keisha

Julie Gordon
Carramar, Australia

Supplies: Cardstock (Bazzill); patterned paper, letters (BasicGrey); chipboard (Maya Road); flowers (Prima); tag (Making Memories); pearls (Kaisercraft); Misc: thread, buttons

There's A Wocket in Uncle's Pocket

Brooke Clark
Simi Valley, CA

Supplies: Patterned paper (Cosmo Cricket, Creative Imaginations, My Mind's Eye, Webster's Pages); letters (American Crafts, Making Memories); foam stamp (Creating Keepsakes); tags (Making Memories); transparent heart (Heidi Swapp); buttons (Fancy Pants); rub-ons (Doodlebug); Misc: pen, adhesive, gloss medium, acrylic paint

Dog Lover

Gretchen McElveen
(Memory Makers Master, 2009)
Helena, AL

Supplies: Patterned paper (BasicGrey, My Mind's Eye); bookplate, brads (7gypsies); letters, rub-ons (Heidi Swapp/Advantus); Misc: pen, ink

Hello Doggie

Keandra Perkins-Willis
New Orleans, LA

Supplies: Cardstock (Papertrey); patterned paper (Reminisce); transparency (Hambly); wood letters (Making Memories); chipboard circle (Scenic Route); stickers (7gypsies, Heidi Swapp); spray mist (Ranger)

Sophie's Legacy

Laura Achilles
Littleton, CO

Supplies: Patterned paper (Jillibean Soup, My Mind's Eye); die-cuts (Jillibean Soup, Jenni Bowlin); letters (American Crafts, Jenni Bowlin); buttons (Nikki Sivils, KI Memories); stick pins, crocheted flower (Fancy Pants); fiber (Martha Stewart Crafts); Misc: ink, cork, punch, rick rack, adhesive

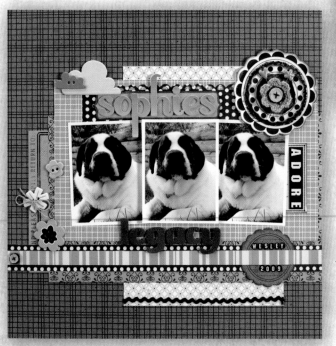

Fall Kitties

Kay Rogers
Midland, MI

Supplies: Cardstock (Bazzill); patterned paper, stickers, felt accents (Little Yellow Bicycle); date sticker (Fontwerks); chipboard letters (BasicGrey); brads (Making Memories); Misc: border punch, pen

His Majesty

Lisa VanderVeen
(Memory Makers Master, 2006)
Santa Monica, CA

Supplies: Software (Adobe Photoshop Elements 7); patterned paper, rub-on borders, sticker by Jen Allyson (Two Peas in a Bucket); quote bubbles by Carina Gardner (Two Peas in a Bucket); letters by Crystal Wilkerson (Jessica Sprague)

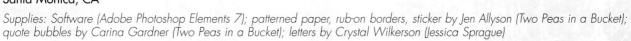

Mitten

Nancy Doren
Colorado Springs, CO

Supplies: Cardstock (Core'dinations); patterned paper (American Crafts, My Mind's Eye); stickers (American Crafts); chipboard hearts (Heidi Swapp/Advantus); Misc: punch, buttons, Batik Regular font

her name is
mitten
(for now)

Officially, her name is Lemony. But we never call her that. She's had so many nicknames over the years, it's hard to keep track. Some of her names are: Kitten. Snoofalette. Babypaw. Honeypaw. Pawbaby. Right now her name happens to be Mitten, but that will probably change in a few months. And we like it that way, because no matter what we call her, she's always our baby.   March 2010

Super Cute

Kristen Jo Simmons
Milton, KY

Supplies: Patterned paper (Prima); chipboard flowers (Peebles); letters (American Crafts); felt accent (Sassafras Lass); pearl (Queen & Co)

super

cute

All Creatures Great and Small

Beth Price
Westfield, IN

Supplies: Patterned paper (My Mind's Eye, Cosmo Cricket, Chatterbox); letters (Chatterbox, My Little Shoebox); trim (Webster's Pages); felt (Prima); scalloped journaling circle (Maya Road); butterflies (Making Memories); Misc: white gel pen, packaging tag

Loving Baby Ty

Angela J. Prieto
Stockton, KS

Supplies: Patterned papers (My Mind's Eye); die-cuts (My Mind's Eye); letters (American Crafts); brads (Inque Boutique); Misc: pen

Cara de Triunfo

Liana Ripa
Betera, Spain

Supplies: Cardstock (Bazzill); patterned paper (SEI); clock faces (Making Memories); letters (BasicGrey); Misc: button, rub-ons, Cricket font

Single-Page Layout Sketches

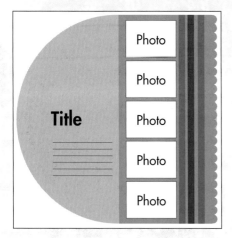

Platinum Pinktallica
Page 12

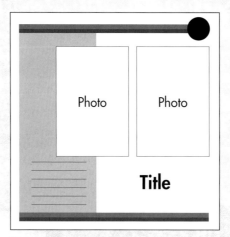

Angel Kisses
Page 13

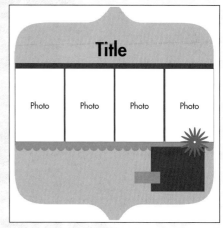

Stain Glass Do-Over
Page 15

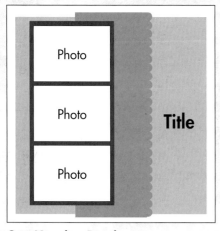

Our Morning Routine
Page 16

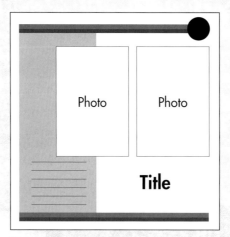

My Little Baker's Man
Page 18

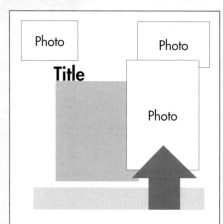

Little Pink Houses
Page 24

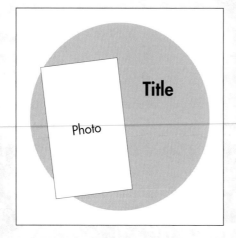

I Believe In . . .
Page 35

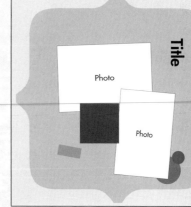

Work Enthusiast
Page 38

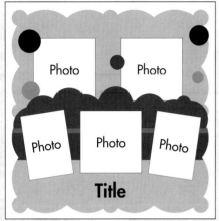

Get Wet
Page 54

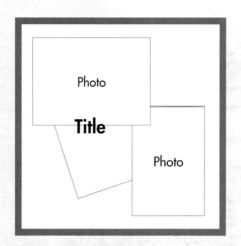

Squeal
Page 58

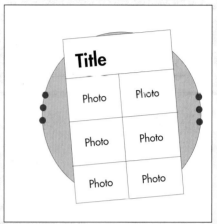

Tractor!
Page 60

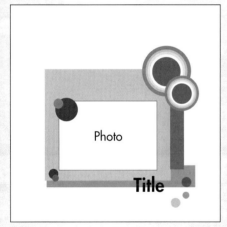

A Perfect Day
Page 61

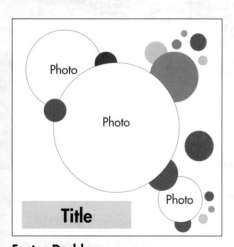

Faster Daddy
Page 63

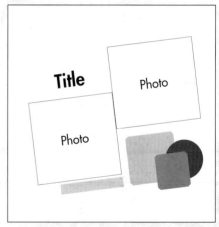

Dude!
Page 65

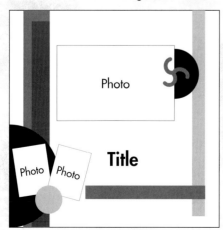

Xtreme Chess, Anyone?
Page 82

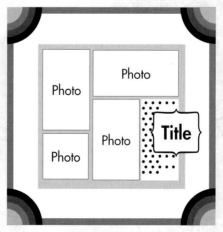

Sunday in San Francisco
Page 91

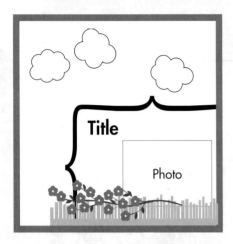

Stop and Smell the Flowers
Page 103

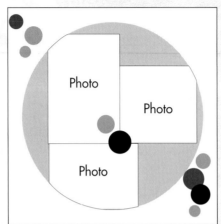

Easter
Page 104

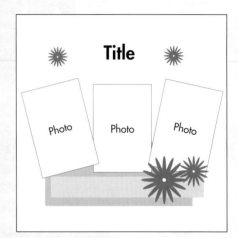

Über Splash of Fun
Page 109

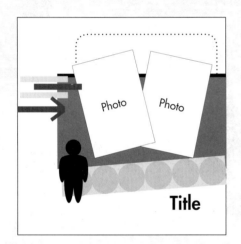

Yum
Page 113

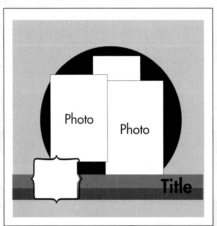

1st Day of 3rd Grade
Page 120

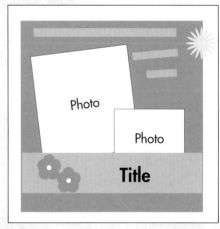

Leaves and Me
Page 124

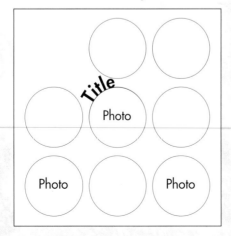

Carve It!
Page 127

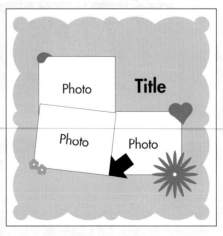

Fun!
Page 133

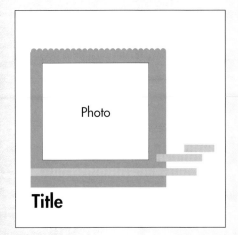

Just Us
Page 160

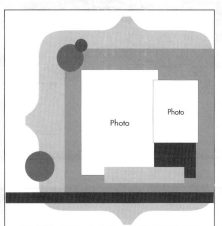

Awesome Mommy
Page 162

As Good As It Gets
Page 166

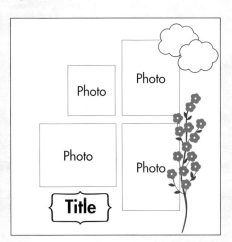

Happiness is Made to be Shared
Page 168

The Good Stuff
Page 172

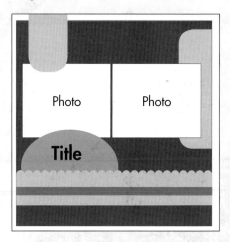

Sweet
Page 173

Tia Lucha
Page 179

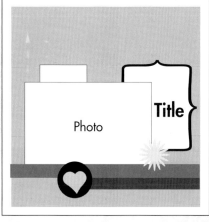

3 Gen
Page 182

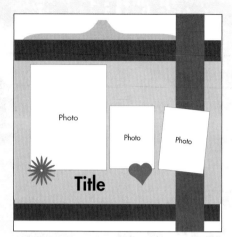

Wild Thing
Page 202

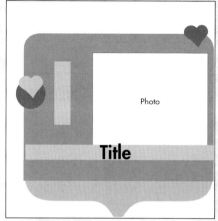

Tiny Hands
Page 208

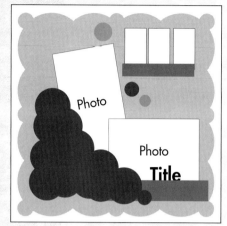

Be Happy
Page 210

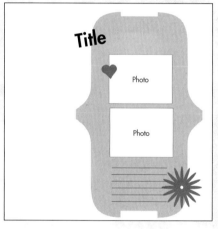

Cookie Mama
Page 212

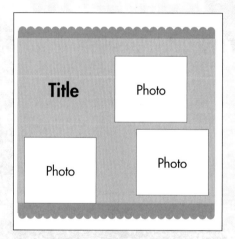

A Loopy Kind of Girl
Page 214

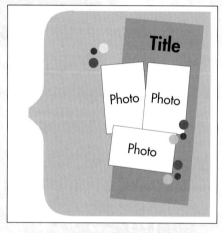

Upside Down Shades
Page 216

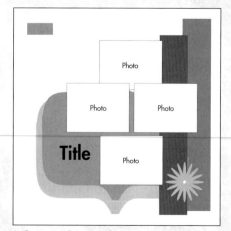

Where's the Beef?
Page 232

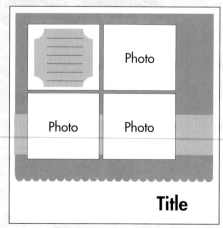

Loving Baby Ty
Page 241

Double-Page Layout Sketches

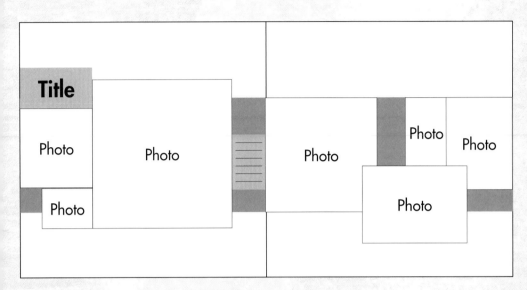

Everyday Life
Page 16

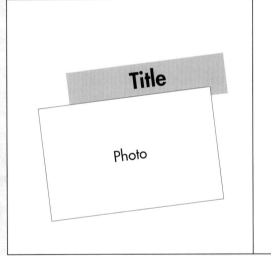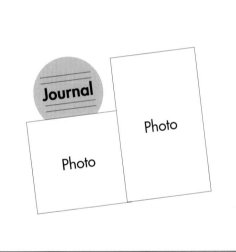

Rocker
Page 49

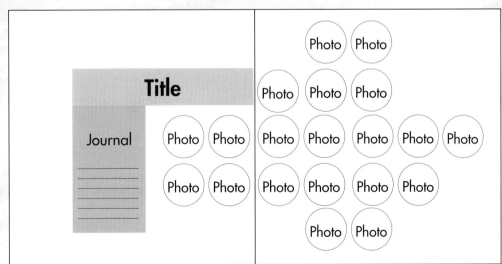

Playtime
Page 68

Boatload of Fun
Page 75

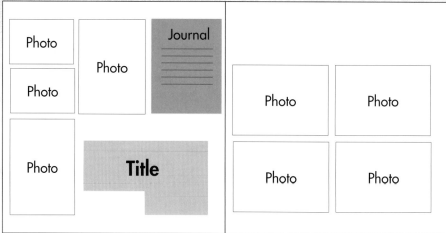

June Tradition
Page 114

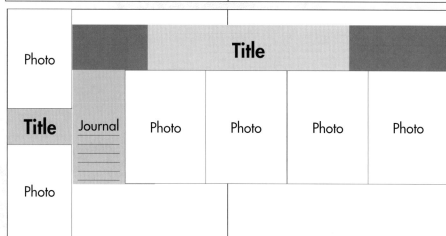

Traditions
Page 138

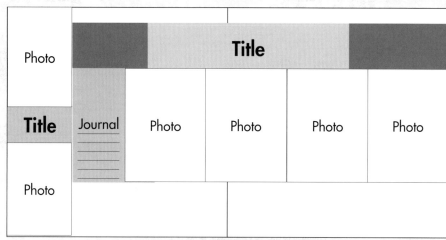

Childhood Girlfriends
Page 183

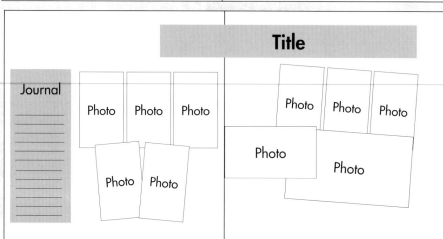

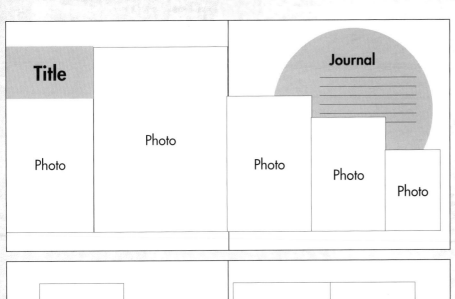

Snow Girl
Page 186

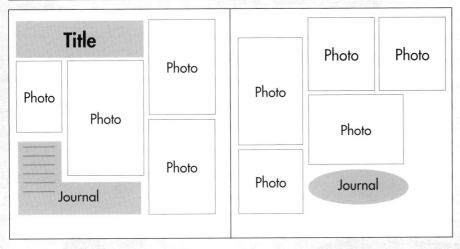

Handmade with Love
Page 203

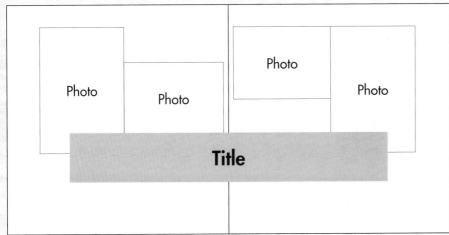

Alexa at 8
Page 207

Source Guide

The following companies manufacture products featured in this book. Please check your local retailers to find these materials, or go to a company's website for the latest product information. In addition, we have made every attempt to properly credit the items mentioned in this book. We apologize to any company that we have listed incorrectly, and we would appreciate hearing from you.

3 Birds Design
(330)-877-9233
www.3birdsdesign.com

3L Scrapbook Adhesives
www.scrapbook-adhesives.com/

3M
(888) 364-3577
www.3m.com

4 heures 37
www.4heures37.com

7gypsies
(877) 749-7797
www.sevengypsies.com

A Muse
(206) 783-4882
www.amuseartstamps.com

A2Z Scraplets
(07) 3885-3355
www.a2zscraplets.com.au

Adirondack Craft
518-302-1891
www.adirondackcraft.com

Adobe Systems Incorporated
(800) 833-6687
www.adobe.com

Adornit / Carolee's Creations
(435) 563-1100
www.adornit.com

Advantus Corp.
(904) 482-0091
www.advantus.com

After Five Designs
www.afterfivedesigns.com

Aja Abney Designs
www.ajaabney.com

Ali Edwards Design
www.aliedwardsdesign.com

All About Scrapbooking
(816) 678-2225
www.aascrapbooking.com

All My Memories
(888) 553-1998
www.allmymemories.com

All Night Media - see Plaid Enterprises

American Crafts
(801) 226-0747
www.americancrafts.com

A Muse
www.amuseartstamps.com

Amy Butler Design
(740) 587-2841
www.amybutlerdesign.com

Amy Hutchinson
http://amy-hutchinson.blogspot.com

Anna Aspnes
http://annaaspnes.typepad.com/

Anna Griffin, Inc.
(888) 87-8170
www.annagriffin.com

ANW Crestwood
(973) 406-5000
www.anwcrestwood.com

Archiver's
www.archiversonline.com

Around The Block
(801) 593-1946
www.aroundtheblockproducts.com

Audrey Neal
http://audneal.typepad.com

Autumn Leaves
(800) 588-6707
www.autumnleaves.com

Avery Dennison Corporation
(800) 462-8379
www.avery.com

BAM POP LLC
www.bampop.com

Banana Frog
www.bananafrog.co.uk

BasicGrey
(801) 544-1116
www.basicgrey.com

Bazzill Basics Paper
(480) 558-8557
www.bazzillbasics.com

Beacon Adhesives
(914) 699-3405
www.beaconadhesives.com

Bella Blvd.
(414) 259-1800
www.bellablvd.net

Berwick Offray, LLC
(800) 344-5533
www.offray.com

Best Creation
www.bestcreation.us

Betsy Tuma
http://www.scrapbookgreen.com

Birch Haberdashery & Crafts
www.birchhaby.com.au

Black Market Paper Society
www.paperaddict.com

Blue Moon Beads
(800) 727-2727
www.creativityinc.com/bluemoonbeads-landing

BoBunny Press
(801) 771-4010
www.bobunny.com

Boxer Scrapbook Productions, LLC
(888) 625-6255
www.boxerscrapbooks.com

Buzz and Bloom
(03) 9584-0132
www.buzzandbloom.net.au

Cardstock Warehouse
www.cardstockwarehouse.com

Carina Gardner
www.carinagardner.com

CatScrap
www.catscrap.com

Catslife Press
(541) 902-7855
www.harborside.com/~catslife/

CD Muckosky
www.cdmuckosky.blogspot.com

Cen's Loft
http://censloft.blogspot.com

Chatterbox, Inc.
(888) 416-6260
www.chatterboxinc.com

Chelley Bean Designs
www.chelleybeandesigns.com

CherryArte
(212) 465-3495
www.cherryarte.com

Claudine Hellmuth
www.claudinehellmuth.com

Clearsnap
(800) 448-4862
www.clearsnap.com

Close To My Heart
(888) 655-6552
www.closetomyheart.com

Cloud 9 Design
(866) 348-5661
www.cloud9design.biz

Cocoa Daisy
(541) 608-0093
www.cocoadaisy.com

Collage Press
(435) 676-2039
www.collagepress.com

COLOP
(43) 7242-66104
www.colop.com

Colörbok, Inc.
(800) 366-4660
www.colorbok.com

Copic
(541) 684-0013
www.copicmarker.com

Core'dinations
www.coredinations.com

Corel
www.corel.com

Cosmo Cricket
(800) 852-8810
www.cosmocricket.com

Couture Cardstock
www.couturecardstock.com

Craft Affair, The
www.thecraftaffair.com

Crafter's Workshop, The
(877) 272-3837
www.thecraftersworkshop.com

Crafty Secrets
(888) 597-8898
www.craftysecrets.com

Crate Paper
(801) 798-8996
www.cratepaper.com

Creating Keepsakes
www.creatingkeepsakes.com

Creative Cafe
www.mycreative-cafe.com

Creative Imaginations
(800) 942-6487
www.cigift.com

Creative Memories
(800) 468-9335
www.creativememories.com

Crystal Wilkerson/Creativity by
Crystal
http://creativitybycrystal.
blogspot.com

D. Reeves Design House
www.dreevesdesignhouse.
blogspot.com

Daily Digi, The
www.thedailydigi.com

Daisy D's Paper Company
(888) 601-8955
www.daisydspaper.com

Darice, Inc.
(800) 321-1494
www.darice.com

Déjà Views
(800) 243-8419
www.dejaviews.com

Design by Dani
www.designbydani.com/store

Designer Digitals
www.designerdigitals.com

Die Cuts With A View
(801) 224-6766
www.diecutswithaview.com

Digichick, The
www.thedigichick.com

Digital Scrapbook Place
(816) 396-5606
www.digitalscrapbookplace.
com

DMC
(973) 589-0606
www.dmc-usa.com

Dollarama
www.dollarama.com

Donna Downey
www.donnadowney.com

Doodlebug Design Inc.
(877) 800-9190
www.doodlebug.ws

Dollarstore, Inc.
(949) 261-7488
www.dollarstore.com

Dreams Inspired
www.dreamsinspired.blogspot.
com

Dream Street Papers
(480) 275-9736
www.dreamstreetpapers.com

Dymo
(800) 426-7827
www.dymo.com

EK Success, Ltd.
(800) 524-1349
www.eksuccess.com

Elle's Studio
(360) 941-6615
www.shopellesstudio.com

Emily Falconbridge (designer)
www.cropperscottage.net

Etsy
www.etsy.com

Evalicious
www.shopevalicious.com

Faber-Castell
www.faber-castell.us

Fancy Pants Designs, LLC
(801) 779-3212
www.fancypantsdesigns.com

Far Flung Craft
(877) 884-7197
www.farflungcraft.com

Fiskars, Inc.
(866) 348-5661
www.fiskars.com

Flair Designs
www.flairdesigns.com

Florileges
www.floriligesdesign.com

FontWerks
(604) 942-3105
www.fontwerks.com

Foof a la
www.foofala.com

Funky Playground Designs
www.funkyplaygrounddesigns.
com

Fynmark
www.fynmark.com.au

Gauche Alchemy
www.gauchealchemy.artfire.
com

gel-a-tins
(800) 393-2151
www.gelatinstamps.com

GCD Studios
www.gcdstudios.com

Girls' Paperie, The
(904) 482-0091
www.thegirlspaperie.com

Glitz Design
(866) 356-6131
www.glitzitnow.com

Glue Dots International (brand)
www.gluedots.com

Go Digital
www.godigitalscrapbooking.
com

Graphic 45
(866) 573-4806
www.g45papers.com

Green Tara
www.greentara.com.au

Hambly Studios
(800) 451-3999
www.hamblystudios.com

Hampton Art Stamps, Inc.
(800) 229-1019
www.hamptonart.com

Harmonie
(450) 681-2519
www.loisirsharmonie.ca

Heidi Grace Designs, Inc.
(866) 348-5661
www.heidigrace.com

Heidi Swapp / Advantus
Corporation
(904) 482-0092
www.heidiswapp.com

Helmar
(612) 9627-4666
www.helmar.com.au

Hero Arts Rubber Stamps, Inc.
(800) 822-4376
www.heroarts.com

Hobby Lobby
www.hobbylobby.com

House of Three
www.houseof3.com

Imagination Project, Inc.
www.imaginationproject.com

Imaginisce
(801) 908-8111
www.imaginisce.com

Inque Boutique
http://stephaniebarnard.
blogspot.com

It Takes Two
(800) 331-9843
www.ittakestwo.com

Jen Allyson
www.theprojectgirl.com

Jenni Bowlin
www.jennibowlin.com

Jessica Sprague
http://spraguelab.square-
space.com

Jillibean Soup
(888) 212-1177
www.jillibean-soup.com

Jo-Ann Stores
www.joann.com

JudiKins
(310) 515-1115
www.judikins.com

Julie Marie Designs
www.juliemariedesigns.com

K&Company
(888) 244-2083
www.kandcompany.com

Kate Hadfield
www.digiscrappingqueen.
com/blog

Kate Teague
www.kate_teague.typepad.com

Katie Pertiet
www.katiepertiet.typepad.com

Kaisercraft
(61) 3-5240-2000
www.kaisercraft.net

Karen Foster Design
(801) 451-9779
www.karenfosterdesign.com

Kelly Panacci
(800) 552-4704
www.kellypanacci.com

Kenner Road
www.kennerroad.com

KI Memories
(972) 243-5595
www.kimemories.com

Kiki Art
(514) 692-4278
www.kiki-art.com

Kitschy Digitals
www.kitschydigitals.com

Kitty Designs
http://a-story-time.blogspot.
com

Kraft Cardstock
www.kraftwarehouse.com

Krystal Hartley
krystalhartley.blogspot.com

La Compagnie du Kraft
www.lacompagniedukraft.fr

La Fourmi Creative
www.lafourmicreative.fr

Lasting Impressions
(801) 298-1983
www.lastingimpressions.com

Lauren Grier Designs
www.scrapfasticdesigns.com

Lefranc & Bourgeois
(02) 4383-8300
www.lefranc-bourgeois.com

Li'l Davis Designs
(480) 223-0080
www.lildavisdesigns.com

Lily Bee Design
(801) 820-6845
www.lilybeedesign.com

Lilypad, The
www.the-lilypad.com

Little Dreamer Designs
www.littledreamerdesigns.com

Lindsay Jane Designs
http://lindsayjanedesigns.
blogspot.com

Love Elsie - see KI Memories

Luxe Designs
(972) 573-2120
www.luxedesigns.com

Lynn Grieveson
www.lynngrieveson.typepad.
com

Magic Mesh
(651) 345-6374
www.magicmesh.com

Magistical Memories
(818) 842-1540
www.magisticalmemories.com

Making Memories
(801) 294-0430
www.makingmemories.com

Manda Girl
www.mandagirl.com

Marah Johnson
http://marah_johnson.typepad.
com

Mark Richards Enterprises, Inc.
(610) 310-4619
www.markrichardsusa.com

Martha Stewart Crafts
www.marthastewartcrafts.com

Marvy Uchida/ Uchida of
America, Corp.
(800) 541-5877
www.uchida.com

May Arts
(800) 442-3950
www.mayarts.com

Maya Road, LLC
(214) 488-3279
www.mayaroad.com

McGill, Inc.
(800) 982-9884
www.mcgillinc.com

Me & My Big Ideas
(949) 583-2065
www.meandmybigideas.com

Melissa Frances/Heart &
Home, Inc.
(888) 616-6166
www.melissafrances.com

Memory Box, Inc.
www.memoryboxco.com

Meredith Fenwick
http://meredithfenwickdesigns.
com/itsallgood

Michaels Arts & Crafts
(800) 642-4235
www.michaels.com

Michelle Coleman
http://mysecondmile.
squarespace.com

Microsoft Corporation
www.microsoft.com

Mindy Terasawa
http://sweetmindy.blogspot.
com

Misty Cato
http://mistycato.wordpress.
com

MultiCraft Imports
(866) 323-9006
www.multicraftimports.com

My Mind's Eye, Inc.
www.mymindseye.com

My Little Shoebox
(510) 397-8890
www.mylittlebox.com

My Little Yellow Bicycle
(860) 286-0244
www.mylyb.com

My Own Creation
www.myowncreation.co.uk

myStamp BOX
www.mystampbox.com

Nichole Heady
http://nicholeheady.typepad.
com

Nicole Crafts
www.nicolecrafts.com

Nikki Sivils
(417) 838-0996
www.nikkisivils.com

NRN Designs
(800) 421-6958
www.nrndesigns.com

October Afternoon
www.octoberafternoon.com

Office Depot
www.officedepot.com

Offray - see Berwick Offray

One Heart…One Mind, LLC
(888) 414-3690

Oriental Trading Company
(800) 875-8480
www.orientaltrading.com

Oscraps
www.oscraps.com

Pageframe Designs
(435) 864-4006
www.pageframedesigns.com

Paislee Press
http://paisleepress.blogspot.
com

Panduro
www.pandurohobby.com

Papemelroti
(632) 375-1069
www.papemelroti.com

Paperchase
www.paperchase.co.uk

Paper Adventures - see ANW
Crestwood

Paper Company, The
(800) 449-1125
www.papercompany.com

Paper Company Studios, The
(973) 406-5000
www.tpcstudios.com

Paper Reflections
(408) 257-5505
www.paperreflections.invita-
tions.com

Paper Source
(888) 727-3711
www.paper-source.com

Paper Studio, The
(480) 557-5700
www.paperstudio.com

Papertrey Ink
www.papertreyink.com

Pattie Knox
http://pattieknox.typepad.com

Pebbles, Inc.
(801) 235-1520
www.pebblesinc.com

Peebles
(800) 743-8730
www.peebles.com

Pelikan
(800) 628-1910
www.pelikan.com

Peppermint Creative
www.peppermintcreative.com

Petaloo
(818) 707-1330
www.petaloo.cameoez.com

Picnik
www.picnik.com

Piggy Tales
(702) 755-8600
www.piggytales.com

Pink Paislee
(816) 729-6124
www.pinkpaislee.com

Pioneer
www.pioneerphotoalbums.com

Plaid Enterprises, Inc.
(800) 842-4197
www.plaidonline.com

Pressed Petals
(800) 748-4656
www.pressedpetals.com

Prima Marketing, Inc.
(909) 627-5532
www.primamarketinginc.com

Prism
www.prismpapers.blogspot.
com

Provo Craft
(800) 937-7686
www.provocraft.com

Purple Cows, Inc.
(877) 386-8264
www.purplecows.net

Purple Onion Designs
www.purpleoniondesigns.com

Queen & Co.
(858) 613-7858
www.queenandcompany.com

Quick Quotes Instant Journaling
(877) 663-7250
www.shopquickquotes.com

QuicKutz, Inc.
(888) 702-1146
www.quickutz.com

Ranger Industries, Inc.
(800) 244-2211
www.rangerink.com

Recollections
www.recollectionsscrapbook.
com

Reminisce Papers
(319) 358-9777
www.shopreminisce.com

Rhonna Farrer Designs
www.rhonnadesigns.com

Riff Raff Designs
www.shopriffraff.blogspot.com

Rob & Bob Studio
http://robandbobstudio.com

Rouge de Garance
www.rougedegarance.com

Rusty Pickle
(801) 746-1045
www.rustypickle.com

Sakura
www.sakuraofamerica.com

Sande Krieger
http://sandekrieger.typepad.
com

Sassafras Lass
(801) 269-1331
www.sassafraslass.com

Sausan Designs
www.sausandesigns.com

Scarlet Lime
www.scarletlime.com

Scenic Route Paper Co.
(801) 225-5754
www.scenicroutepaper.com

ScrapArtist
(734) 717-7775
www.scrapartist.com

Scrapbook-Bytes
(509) 209-9414
www.scrapbook-bytes.com

Scrapbook Graphics
www.scrapbookgraphics.com

Scrap Girls
(866) 598-3444
www.scrapgirls.com

Scrap Orchard
www.scraporchard.com

Scrapworks, LLC
(801) 363-1010
www.scrapworks.com

Scrap Within Reach
(602) 758-5262
www.scrapwithinreach.com

Scrapbook In Style TV
www.scrapinstyletv.com

Scrappin' Sports Stuff
www.scrappinstuff.com

Scribble Scrabble LLC
(801) 400-9741
www.scribblescrabble.net

SEI, Inc.
(800) 333-3279
www.shopsei.com

Shabby Miss Jenn Designs
www.shabbymissjenndesigns.
com

Shabby Princesswww.shabby-
princess.com

Shawna Clingerman
www.mylittlescraps.com

Shimmerz
(208) 880-7693
www.shimmerz.com

Silhouette
www.silhouettemachine.com

Sizzix
(877) 355-4766
www.sizzix.com

Some Odd Girl
www.someoddgirl.com

Something Blue Studios
www.somethingbluestudios.com

Spellbinders
(888) 547-0400
www.spellbinderspaperarts.
com

S.R.M. Press, Inc.
(310) 306-1595
www.srmpress.com

Stacy Towers
http://sjtowers.blogspot.com

Stampendous
(800) 869-0474
www.stampendous.com

Stampin' Up!
(800) 782-6787
www.stampinup.com

Stampotique
(602) 862-0237
www.stampotique.com

Stamps by Judith
www.stampsbyjudith.com

Staples, Inc.
www.staples.inc

StazOn—see Tsukineko

Stemma / Masterpiece Studios
www.masterpiecestudios.com

Sticky Thumb, The
(435) 994-0021
www.thestickythumb.com

Studio 18
www.studiojewel.blogspot.com

Studio Calico
(270) 721-2921
www.studiocalico.com

Sueli Cobert Designs
www.suelicolbert.blogspot.com

Sweet Shoppe Designs
www.sweetshoppedesigns.com

Sweet Vintage 78
www.etsy.com/shop/
sweetvintage 78

Sweetwater
(800) 359-3094
www.sweetwaterscrapbook.
com

Syndee Nuckles
http://soshesaid.typepad.com

Tanya Leigh Designs
www.tanyaleigh.wordpress.
com

Tangie Baxter Designs
www.tangiebaxter.com

Tattered Angels
(970) 622-9677
www.mytatteredangels.com

Technique Tuesday
(503) 644-4073
www.techniquetuesday.com

Teresa Collins Designs
(877) 417-3195
www.teresecollinsdesigns.com

Therm O Web
http://www.thermoweb.com

Three Bugs in a Rug, LLC
(801) 804-6657
www.threebugsinarug.com

Three Paper Peonies
www.threepaperpeonies.
blogspot.com

Tia Bennett
www.tiabennett.typepad.com

Tim Holtz
www.timholtz.com

Tinkering Ink
(435) 563-6784
www.tinkeringink.com

Toga Createur d'Envies
www.toga-le-site.com

Tombow
www.tombowusa.com

Tonic Studios
(608) 836-4478
www.tonic-studios.com

Trends International
www.trendsinternational.com

Tsukineko
(425) 883-7733
www.tsukineko.com

Two Little Pixels
www.twolittlepixels.com

Two Peas in a Bucket
(888) 896-7327
www.twopeasinabucket.com

Uni-ball
www.uniball-na.com

Unity Stamp Company
(320) 354-4450
www.unitystampco.com

Upsy Daisy Designs
(250) 881-8779
www.upsydaisydesigns.com

Vandoros
www.vandoros.com

Vinnie Pearce
http://vinniepearce.typepad.
com

Wal-Mart
www.walmart.com

Want 2 Scrap
(260) 740-2976
www.want2scrap.com

We R Memory Keepers, Inc.
(801) 539-5000
www.weronthenet.com

Webster's Pages
(800) 543-6104
www.websterspages.com

Wackadoo Stamping
www.wackadoostamping.
blogspot.com

WorldWin Papers
(888) 843-6455
www.worldwinpapers.com

Wrights Ribbon Accents
(877) 597-4448
www.wrights.com

Wyla, Inc.
(904) 886-4338
www.wyla.com

Xyron
(800) 793-3523
www.xyron.com

Zoe Pearn Designs
www.zoepearndesigns.com

Zutter
(877) 273-2818
www.binditall.com

Zva Creative
(801) 243-9281
www.zvacreative.com

Index of Contributors

254

Index

More Scrapbook Ideas and Inspiration!

Start Scrapbooking

Your Essential Guide to Recording Memories

Wendy Smedley

Packed with everything you need to know to dive into the craft, *Start Scrapbooking* shows you can have fun and scrap in simple ways. Along with more than 100 fresh layout ideas, you'll find all the essentials for getting started and staying on track. Find your starting point, then design layouts following basic principles. Plus, you'll love a gallery of theme ideas for scrapping every occasion. Perfect for beginners looking to get started as well as any scrapbooker looking for simple ideas, *Start Scrapbooking* will help you record your memories with ease.

hardcover with concealed wire-o binding; 8" × 10"; 128 pages

ISBN-10: 1-59963-128-8

ISBN-13: 978-1-59963-128-8

SRN: Z6656

Scrapbook PageMaps 2

More Sketches for Creative Layouts and Cards

Becky Fleck

Even the most imaginative people get stumped sometimes. Discover new layout sketches and artwork from the author of *Scrapbook PageMaps*, including a full chapter devoted to greeting cards. Learn to use sketches to focus and coordinate your ideas whenever you're feeling overwhelmed by materials, photos and journaling. Included are 64 travel-size sketch cards for easy planning wherever you get inspired. If you're feeling stumped, *Scrapbook PageMaps 2* will help you tell your story!

hardcover with concealed wire-o binding; 8.25" × 10.875"; 160 pages

ISBN-10: 1-59963-117-2

ISBN-13: 978-1-59963-117-2

SRN: Z5018

Remember This

Fresh Page Ideas to Scrapbook the Year

Kimber McGray and Summer Fullerton

It's not hard to remember the big events: birthdays, holidays, vacations, graduation. The hard part is finding creative ways to scrapbook the same activities year after year. With 150 fresh layout ideas from a variety of contributors, authors Kimber McGray and Summer Fullerton will inspire you to create your own creative layouts during every season. With pages featuring multiple photos, people of all ages, and a variety of events and activities, there's something for every scrapbooker!

paperback; 8.25" × 10.875"; 128 pages

ISBN-10: 1-59963-091-5

ISBN-13: 978-1-59963-091-5

SRN: Z3842

These and other fine Memory Makers titles are available at your local craft retailer, bookstore or online supplier, or visit our website at www.mycraftivitystore.com.

Five reasons to visit

www.memorymakersmagazine.com

1. Download FREE projects

2. Get expert advice

3. Connect with other scrappers

4. Sign up for weekly e-inspiration

5. Find the latest news, inspiration, tips and ideas